QUEEN VICTORIA WAS AMUSED

QUEEN VICTORIA WAS AMUSED

Alan Hardy

TAPLINGER PUBLISHING COMPANY
NEW YORK

7-28-78

FOR BETTY

19322

First published in the United States in 1977 by
TAPLINGER PUBLISHING CO., INC.
New York, New York

© 1976 by Alan Hardy
All rights reserved.
Printed in Great Britain

Library of Congress Catalog Card Number: 76-55035
ISBN 0-8008-6566-9

Contents

CONTENTS

Illustrations

❈

Acknowledgments

I wish to express my thanks to Her Majesty the Queen for gracious permission to quote from Queen Victoria's Journal and other papers in the Royal Archives, and to reproduce pictures and photographs in the Royal Collection.

I am also grateful to the following for permission to quote from the published works indicated:

Sir Rupert Hart-Davis, *The Letters of Oscar Wilde*; the literary executor of the late Hector Bolitho; Mr. A. R. Mills, *The Halls of Ravenswood* and *Two Victorian Ladies*; Mr. Edward Boykin, *Victoria, Albert and Mrs. Stevenson*.

Evans Brothers Ltd., *My Memories of Six Reigns* by H.H. Princess Marie Louise, *For My Grandchildren* by H.R.H. Princess Alice Countess of Athlone, *Regina v Palmerston* by John Connell, and *Dearest Child, Dearest Mama* and *Your Dear Letter* edited by Roger Fulford; Macmillan London and Basingstoke, *The Greville Memoirs* edited by Lytton Strachey and Roger Fulford, and *Henry Ponsonby, His Life and Letters* by Arthur Ponsonby; John Murray Ltd., *The Letters of Queen Victoria, Creevey's Life and Times* by John Gore, *Mary Ponsonby, A Memoir* edited by Magdalen Ponsonby, *Life with Queen Victoria* by Sir Victor Mallet, and *The Queen thanks Sir Howard* by M. E. McLintock; Methuen and Co. Ltd., *My Early Life* by ex-Emperor William II, and *Gladstone to His Wife* by A. Tilney Bassett; William Collier, *Queen Victoria at Windsor and Balmoral* by James Pope-Hennessy.

Cassell Collier Macmillan and Charles Scribner's Sons, *The Story of My Life* by Queen Marie of Roumania; Weidenfeld and Nicolson Ltd and Harper and Row, *Victoria R.I.* by Elizabeth Longford; Weidenfeld and Nicolson and Macmillan Publishing

Co. Inc, *Rosebery* by Robert Rhodes James; Eyre and Spottiswoode Ltd. and St. Martin's Press Inc., *Disraeli* by Robert Blake; The Bodley Head and Houghton Mifflin Co., *The Empress Brown* by Tom Cullen; Phaidon and Co. Ltd. and Praeger Publishers Inc., *The Russians* by Leonid Vladimirov; Cassell Collier Macmillan, *The English Empress* by E. C. Corti.

Anthony Shiel Associates, Macmillans and Associated University Presses, *Dear and Honoured Lady* edited by Hope Dyson and Charles Tennyson; David Higham Associates, *The Reign of Queen Victoria* by Hector Bolitho; A. D. Peters and Co., *The Life and Times of Lord Mountbatten* by John Terraine; Curtis Brown Ltd., *Lady Lytton's Court Diary* edited by Mary Lutyens, *Cosmo Gordon Lang* by J. G. Lockhart, *Chapters of Life* by Sir Charles Petrie, and *Recollections of Three Reigns* by Sir Frederick Ponsonby.

Jonathan Cape Ltd., *Letters of Lady Augusta Stanley* and *Later Letters of Lady Augusta Stanley* edited by Hector Bolitho and A. Baillie; Frederick Muller Ltd., *Hessian Tapestry* by David Duff; Gerald Duckworth and Co., *Queen Victoria* by Arthur Ponsonby; Hutchinson Publishing Group Ltd., *Queen Victoria's John Brown* by E. E. P. Tisdall; Oxford University Press, *Randall Davidson* by G. K. A. Bell; Constable and Co., *Max* by David Cecil, and *C.B.: A Life of Sir Henry Campbell-Bannerman* by John Wilson; Longmans Group Ltd., *The Life and Letters of Lord Macaulay* by Sir George Otto Trevelyan; Ernest Benn Ltd., *The Letters of Disraeli to Lady Bradford and Lady Chesterfield* edited by the Marquess of Zetland.

The Estate of Lady Gwendolen Cecil, *The Life and Times of Robert Marquess of Salisbury* by Lady Gwendolen Cecil; the Estate of E. F. Benson, *As We Were* by E. F. Benson; and the Society of Authors as Literary Representative of Sir Compton Mackenzie, *My Life and Times* by Compton Mackenzie.

Finally, I would like to place on record my gratitude to my wife for enormous encouragement and infinite patience.

May 1976   ALAN HARDY

The Golden Thread

By reason of her position, long life and force of personality Queen Victoria bestrode the nineteenth century. Nevertheless, if a poll were to be taken to find out what is now generally known about her a large number of replies would indicate only that she uttered those dreadful words 'We are not amused'. For over half a century this phrase has hung like a millstone round the neck of her reputation. It has damned Victoria as 'Let them eat cake' damned Marie Antoinette. Now one of the greatest clichés in the English language, it has left in the mind of millions the impression of a puritanical old she-dragon breathing fire and brimstone.

My original idea when I started work on this book was simply to bring together in one volume some of the funny stories connected with the Queen, in an attempt to demonstrate that there was a lighter, gayer side to her life. The need to extend my scope emerged as my researches got under way. For the deeper I delved the more I became convinced that this lighter side was in fact the lynch-pin that held together her whole personality.

To put it another way: a widely-embracing sense of humour, a love of simple pleasures and a tremendous capacity for being amused run through the Queen's life like a golden thread. By following this thread it becomes easy to link together the eager young girl, the intensely happy married woman, the withdrawn widow and the formidable Grandmother of Europe. No longer need there be a tendency to regard them as four different people. It becomes clear, for instance, that the matriarch's formidableness is only a layer of varnish superimposed on the simple girlishness and naïveté still remaining underneath. Indeed, what becomes most striking is not that Queen Victoria changed so much in the course of a long life, but that she changed so little. The breadth of her sense of humour is there throughout—ranging from a child-like ability to be diverted by slapstick, farces and circuses, through a taste for risqué stories and broad jokes, to an appreciation of dry subtle humour, wit and mimicry and a gift for repartee.

This is not to deny the existence of another, darker side of the Queen's nature—her intense interest in deaths and funerals, for example, and her proneness to excessive mourning (partly due, no doubt, to the grafting of the Coburg melancholy on to the excessive sentimentality of the Hanoverians). In old age, especially, she could, like many other old ladies, be sullen, stubborn and selfish. No-one was more conscious of her imperfections than she was herself. 'I will daily pray for God's help to improve' is typical of the New Year resolutions she continued to set herself.

In the make-up of her personality, as in everyone else's, there was light and shade. The truth is that throughout her life the lugubrious side went hand in hand with the light-hearted, the tragic with the comic muse. 'The Queen,' noted a keen observer of her old age, 'is either very serious or all smiles.' Since her death, with the help of the all-pervading 'We are not amused', her serious aspects have, in my view, been the subject of excessive attention. Yet not to take full account of the smiles is to mis-understand a complex personality.

I therefore make no excuse for setting out deliberately to re-dress the balance by highlighting the lighter side of the Queen's nature. Too much has been written already about the gloom and the storms in her life, not enough about the fact that, in spite of everything, the sunshine in her nature persistently shone through.

Once the, hitherto damning, 'We are not amused' has been put in its proper perspective, this book is about the sunshine.

PART ONE

Why We were not Amused

Why We were not Amused

During the later years of Queen Victoria's life the saying most commonly associated with her was her childhood promise 'I will be good'. The period following her death saw the growth of twentieth-century prejudices against all things Victorian. It was in those years that the 'We are not amused' of her old age gradually took pride of place in the public mind. There was, however, for long an air of mystery about how this devastating phrase came into existence. Reference book researchers looking for an explanation fell back on *The Notebooks of a Spinster Lady* published anonymously in 1919. Much of this book had been written during the last years of the Queen's life by someone who moved in London society but who heard royal gossip at only second or third hand. The solution it offered involved the telling of an improper story.

> After dinner the Queen makes herself agreeable putting things in a quaint original way with a great deal of humour and a most musical laugh . . . But her remarks can freeze as well as crystallise. There is a tale of the unfortunate equerry who ventured during dinner at Windsor to tell a story with a spice of scandal or impropriety in it. 'We are not amused', said the Queen when he had finished.

> Another explanation that went around was to the effect that Queen Victoria had been provoked by a distasteful piece of mimicry. The offender, someone suggested, was 'the unfortunate Admiral Maxse—Queen Victoria commanded that he should give his well-known imitation of her august self, watched him put a handkerchief on his head and blow out his cheeks, said in her iciest tone "We are not amused" and left him worse than dead'. The daughter of the 'unfortunate Admiral' protested. 'My father,' she

pointed out, 'never imitated anyone in his life and I doubt if he ever spoke to Queen Victoria.' Nevertheless the suggestion that mimicry was involved was widely accepted.

A bit more research would have unearthed the fact that 'We are not amused', and another explanation for it, had actually appeared in print during the old Queen's lifetime. In his *Popular Royalty*, published at the time of the Diamond Jubilee, Arthur Beavan had this to say:

> Her Majesty, like all her children, has a keen sense of humour and a ready wit. But if a joke be not strictly within the bounds of decorum, she can, and does, allow the dignity of her exalted position to assert itself, as the following anecdotes will show.
>
> Once the Queen heard some gentlemen laughing so loudly at the other end of the room over something one of the party had just related, that she walked across to where they stood, and said, 'I should like to hear that joke Captain —. It must be very amusing'. Captain — flushed, looked much confused and asked to be exempted from repeating it. The Queen insisted, and the most unfortunate captain, losing his presence of mind, gave it verbatim. It was *not* a lady's joke, and the Queen with much dignity and *hauteur* remarked, 'We are not at all pleased'.
>
> On another occasion, when a number of the Queen's grand-children, who were visiting her, had got together in their room one of them made a joke which raised such roars of laughter, that Her Majesty entered their apartment to know the cause of so much merriment. The joke was somewhat 'advanced', and the young people had to be asked more than once before they could be persuaded to repeat it. But a Queen's command must be obeyed; so the boldest spirit—a masculine one—related it; whereupon Her Majesty drew herself up in dignified rebuke, and with the words 'We are not amused!' left the room.

'Laughter always seems to excite the Queen's curiosity' was Beavan's mild comment as he launched her disastrous words on to a sea of print.

It was not till seventy years later that a more authoritative account appeared. As was well known in his family, the man who had provoked the Queen had been the Honourable Alexander Yorke, Groom-in-waiting during the last sixteen years of her reign. In 1968 Yorke's great-nephew Sir Victor Mallet published some family letters. In his introduction Mallet accepted the mimicry version of the story. The Queen, he pointed out, 'had a definite sense of fun, but her sense of humour was limited, as Alick Yorke was to learn only too well from the much-quoted "We are not amused", after he had—against his will, and under royal command —given one of his mimicry performances'.

Then, almost as an afterthought, Mallet went on to recount Alick Yorke's *own* explanation of what had happened:

> Another niece of Alick's, Lady Susan Birch, often related a different version of the story as given her by Alick himself. During a dinner party at Windsor Alick was sitting next to a German to whom he told a slightly risqué story. The German guffawed so loudly that the Queen asked Alick to tell her what had caused such mirth. Alick thereupon repeated the story and received the classic snub.

The question that now poses itself is: why not accept Alick Yorke's explanation as the true one? After all he had good reason for sticking to the truth. As he survived Queen Victoria by only ten years there were undoubtedly living at the time of his death a number of people who had witnessed the incident and could vouch for what had happened.

To support Yorke's explanation there is ample evidence that Queen Victoria had sharp ears and was a keen listener to what was said at her dinner table. She never liked to miss a joke or interesting conversation. As she well knew, Alick Yorke could be very amusing. Alick himself once recounted to a fellow-courtier an example of her breaking in on his dinner-table conversation:

> Alick Yorke told me that at dinner he talked to his neighbour about Queen Mary, daughter of Henry VIII, and Her Majesty heard the word Queen and asked which Queen he was talking about. When he told her she replied, 'Oh! my bloody ancestor'.

Moreover, foreign visitors were frequent guests at the Queen's table. The idea of her attention being drawn to Alick Yorke by loud German guffaws accordingly has a ring of truth about it. In my view one has, therefore, to accept Yorke's account of the risqué story as the true cause of 'We are not amused'.

The next question that has to be answered is why did Queen Victoria react in so devastating a fashion? Normally no-one loved an amusing story more than she. Risqué or otherwise, in the right circumstances she would be the first to laugh. Perhaps she was simply in an off-mood that evening. A more likely explanation is that she was embarrassed—embarrassed at having herself demanded, within the hearing of young unmarried ladies, the retailing of a story which turned out to be indelicate.

A clue to the circumstances is provided by her use of the word 'we'. This indicates her inclusion of others present in presumed joint displeasure rather than an uncharacteristic use of the royal 'we'. Her difficulty was that, though she personally had a partiality for quite broad jokes, she had always regarded it as her paramount duty to retain decorum at Court. She took particularly seriously her duty of safeguarding the morals of young unmarried women under her roof. Whether they were her own relations or the Maids of Honour, she looked upon herself as *in loco parentis*.

Sir Henry Ponsonby, her Private Secretary for many years, was present on one occasion when the Queen nearly forgot herself. Her youngest daughter, Princess Beatrice, was twenty-one when a guest started talking about the manners of Americans of an earlier generation.

> One of them, he told the Queen at dinner, had said to his English hostess: 'How old are you? How long have you been married? I should like to see your nuptual bed.' The Queen bursts out laughing but raised her napkin to protect Princess Beatrice and the Maids of Honour who sat on the other side of of the table.

Years later her granddaughter Marie Louise recounted another instance of the Queen's 'deliciously old-world' protective instinct.

It is one which, incidentally, reveals her real opinion of Alick Yorke. Princess Helena Victoria wanted to arrange a picnic at Balmoral and submitted a list of those who would be going.

> . . . Grandmama scrutinised this list of most charming but not very exciting invites to the picnic, and said to each 'Yes'. But when she came to Alick Yorke's name she added, 'Yes, Alick's quite safe!' Alick was enraged when he was told he was quite safe to squire a party of elderly ladies!

In fact they were not all elderly: Princess Helena Victoria herself was a young unmarried woman.

If it is taken into account that Queen Victoria regarded it as her duty to act as a mother hen, it becomes easy to understand her horror when she was involved in the broadcasting at her dinner table of something indelicate. In such circumstances she had to react pretty smartly. So, with a cutting remark, she quickly put an end to the conversation and checked any ribald laughter.

That her remark had no more significance than an embarrassed cover-up is confirmed by the fact that Alick Yorke's position and popularity at Court were in no way affected. Throughout the rest of the Queen's life he was both much in demand and greatly appreciated. He was an unusual combination of the highly respectable and the highly comic. His background was impeccable. A son of the fourth Earl of Hardwicke, he came from a family long connected with the Court and held in affectionate regard by Queen Victoria. Originally he had been in the Household of Prince Leopold, the Queen's youngest son, whom he had met up at Oxford. On Leopold's death in 1884 Victoria appointed him to her own Household and kept him with her till her death.

Yorke's theatrical leanings, acting ability and comic qualities had already earned him a unique position at Court. He had become known as the unofficial 'Master of the Revels' and was the nearest thing Queen Victoria had to a Court Jester. His great-nephew, Victor Mallet, remembered him as a most unusual courtier altogether:

> Alick Yorke would from his appearance be described nowadays

as an elderly pansy, though he seems to have been the kindest and most virtuous of men, and no breath of scandal ever passed his way. He had sparkling eyes, an inquisitive nose, and brown hair neatly brushed and oiled. His figure was short and rotund. He was talkative and witty, and a great amateur actor who organised the Queen's theatricals—a feature of Court life for the younger members of the Royal Family. He dressed in an extravagant manner, with huge buttonholes, jewelled rings and tie-pins. I can remember the whiff of scent that accompanied his entrance into a room.

As a small boy I always looked forward to this godfather's visits; and when ogres were my ruling passion he would growl and act the ogre till my brother and I were in fits of laughter. In an old newspaper cutting I find him described as a great personal favourite of the Queen's and the organiser of all the Court theatricals and *tableaux vivants*. A first-rate amateur actor, he has enormous acquaintance among interesting people of all ranks, tells excellent anecdotes and gives charming bachelor dinners.

Alick's permanent popularity with Queen Victoria was vouched for at the time by his niece Marie. As Miss Adeane she joined the Royal Household in 1888 as a Maid of Honour and was soon sending home accounts like the following of the progress of her uncle:

> He shines tremendously when in Waiting and makes things pleasant for all the Household suggesting walks and rides and always including the Ladies . . . As for the Queen, she invariably sends for him after dinner and we have comic songs, etc. Last night he did 'The Pigs', and 'Sleepy Song' and most of his imitations, the evenings really quite cheery and I am sure it does the Queen good to laugh.

On at least one occasion, according to E. F. Benson, the Queen herself joined Yorke in song:

> Once, when she was quite an old woman, she suddenly made

the portentous announcement to Alick Yorke who was in waiting, that after lunch he and she would sing duets. Someone sat down at the piano to play the accompaniment, and the Queen propped up on the table between the two vocalists a copy of Gilbert and Sullivan's opera *Patience*, and found the place.

She said, 'Now, Mr. Yorke, you begin,' and Mr. Yorke obediently sang to the Queen, 'Prithee, pretty maiden, will you marry me?'. He got through his verse fairly well, and then the Queen in a very clear soft voice sang, 'Gentle Sir, although to marry I'm inclined'. She was much pleased with herself, and stopped in the middle of her verse to say, 'You know, Mr. Yorke, I was taught singing by Mendelssohn'.

One of the Queen's granddaughters, over from Germany on a visit in 1889, confirms Yorke's popularity with the old lady. 'Yesterday after dinner Mr. Yorke sang and performed a little, he was most amusing and witty,' ran one of her letters to her mother; 'Grandmama laughed till she was red in the face just the way you do.' During the same visit Yorke's abilities as an actor and producer came into play when the Queen decided that, to keep her granddaughter amused, there should be amateur theatricals. In consequence, as she herself told the girl's mother, 'we were kept in fits of laughter'.

Vicky has a decided turn for acting and Mr. Yorke was inimitable, as he always is. As the little piece only took half an hour, Mr. Yorke afterwards gave us his killingly funny 'Picnic', which I had not heard again for seven or eight years, and which was as clever as ever.

Shortly after this Alick Yorke went on a trip to the Far East. He was sadly missed. 'Her Majesty,' Marie Adeane reported, 'was so pleased to hear that Uncle Alick was so near on his way home.' After his return to duty Marie resigned her own post in order to marry Bernard Mallet. A few years later she returned to Court as a Woman of the Bedchamber. She found her Uncle, together with the amateur theatricals, as popular as ever. 'Uncle Alick always convulses everybody whenever he puts his head on the stage.' When Yorke was taking part in a production 'the zest with which the Queen entered the fun' was particularly noticed.

Marie Mallet was a confidante of Queen Victoria right up to the end of the reign, and her accounts of Court life make it clear that her Uncle Alick too remained a favourite to the end.

It is, therefore, obvious that, regardless of the emphasis posterity has seen fit to place on 'We are not amused', its actual effect at the time was practically nil, no more than a tiny ripple on a tranquil sea. Because of his very ability to amuse Alick Yorke continued to play an important part in Court life. For he helped satisfy that part of Queen Victoria's nature which craved for simple amusement—something which, as will be seen, had survived the endurance test of her childhood and remained with her all her life.

PART TWO

Why We were Amused

CHAPTER I

The Gilded Cage

My earliest recollections are connected with Kensington Palace, where I can remember crawling on a yellow carpet spread out for that purpose—and being told that if I cried and was naughty my 'Uncle Sussex' would hear me and punish me, for which reason I always screamed when I saw him!

It was thus that Queen Victoria was to record her earliest childhood memory. An unusual childhood it certainly had been, for she had hardly entered the world, 'as plump as a partridge', a veritable 'pocket Hercules', when her father quitted it. Although regarded as the most robust of the sons of King George III he was taken ill while staying with his family at Sidmouth and was dead within a few days. The year was 1820, Victoria, his only child, was eight months old. She returned to London to be brought up by her mother, the Duchess of Kent, a German princess now widowed for a second time. Life was spent in a grace-and-favour apartment at Kensington Palace. It was a thoroughly female *ménage*. The only male figure of importance was her mother's brother Leopold who became King of the Belgians when Victoria was eleven. It was only through his financial assistance that the Duchess of Kent was able to remain in England and bring up her child in any degree of comfort. Even so, money was short and the young princess was brought up simply and quietly.

It soon became apparent that she was an affectionate and high-spirited child. The aged William Wilberforce was one of the first to succumb to her charm. 'In consequence of a very civil message from the Duchess of Kent, I waited on her this morning,' he informed Hannah More. 'She received me with her fine animated child on the floor by her side, with its playthings, of which I soon became one.' But bishops, who in those days still wore powdered wigs, were less assured of a welcome. As Victoria herself remembered, 'I had a great horror of Bishops on account of their wigs and aprons'. Among the many characteristics of the mature Queen that can be traced back to early childhood this was clearly one: all her life she had a barely-concealed distaste for bishops.

Her first teacher noticed a number of other traits that were to prove permanent—her curiosity, her honesty, her natural exuberance, her gift for repartee. He kept a diary cataloging her progress, beginning just before her fourth birthday.

> April 16th 1823. The Duchess seems very anxious for the improvement of her little daughter, and had promised a reward if she said a good lesson. The Princess asked for the reward before she began the lesson.
>
> May 20th 1823. When I came away dinner had just been announced to the little Princess. I said I hoped she would be good, and that she would attend to her book and read a good lesson. 'Yes' she said, 'and I will eat a good dinner.'

Certainly the accounts which survive of the future Queen's early life, in what was then leafy, suburban Kensington, paint a picture of a tranquil, cared-for existence. There is even a fairy-tale quality in evidence in the early memories of Leigh Hunt, more often a critic of royalty.

> A magnificent footman in scarlet came behind her, with the splendidest pair of calves in white stockings which we ever beheld. He looked like a giant fairy, personating for his little lady's sake the grandest kind of footman he could think of; and his calves seemed to have been made out of a couple of the biggest chain lamps in the possession of the godmother of Cinderella.

In reality all was not as tranquil as it seemed. The Princess could be very strong-willed and downright even at this stage in her life.

The Duchess of Kent's task was no easy one. She deserves particular praise for preventing her daughter from having inflated ideas about her station, for imparting excellent manners and for curbing the child's more headstrong tendencies. That Victoria grew up to be a Queen with many good qualities owes something to her mother's tight rein in her early years. The Duchess's main mistake was to fall completely under the influence of the ambitious and scheming Comptroller of her Household, an Irish adventurer named John Conroy. His wish was to secure power for himself when the Princess came to the throne. This led to an increasingly strict regime at Kensington as Duchess and Comptroller endeavoured to bend the growing girl's will to their own. The fact that they failed speaks volumes for Victoria's strength of character. That her high spirits and sense of humour did not wither away during these years, but simply went underground to emerge at the first opportunity, is also indicative of great durability. They were to prove equally durable in surviving other storms.

It is, however, important to remember that it was not until Victoria was in her teens that she was fully aware that the regime was constricting and that discord developed between mother and daughter. It is true that as a child she was often lonely, particularly after her half-sister Feodore, a child of her mother's first marriage, married and left home. But thrown on her own resources she made the best of her position with that adaptability which children possess. Just before her ninth birthday Mrs. Arbuthnot found her 'quite playful and childish playing with her dolls and in high spirits'. These dolls developed into a large collection (still preserved) and on them she lavished great devotion. She and her governess Baroness Lehzen dressed over a hundred. Many were characters from operas and ballets that the Princess had seen. Asked in old age whether she had liked dolls as a child, Queen Victoria waxed enthusiastic. 'The Queen has no hesitation in saying that she was quite devoted to dolls and played with them till she was fourteen. Her favourites were small ones and small wooden ones which could be dressed as she liked and had a house.'

During the years she was growing up she was moving higher in the line of succession to the throne. By the time Victoria was eight only her Uncle William remained between her and the throne. At about this time, somewhat to her mother's trepidation, the Princess left her ivory tower for a short while to enjoy her first real taste of Court life, albeit the somewhat Bohemian existence that George IV led at Windsor. From the time the old roué greeted his niece with 'Give me your little paw', he was captivated by her vivacity. The wide-eyed child was even more delighted with her first peep into a new and exciting way of life. Years later she described with relish the pleasure it gave her.

> I was driven about the Park and taken to Sandpit Gate where the King had a menagerie—with wapitis, gazelles, chamois, etc, etc. Then we went (I think the next day) to Virginia Water and met the King in his phaeton in which he was driving with the Duchess of Gloucester—and he said 'Pop her in', and I was lifted in and placed between him and Aunt Gloucester, who held me round the waist. (Mamma was much frightened) I was greatly pleased. . . . We drove round the nicest part of Virginia Water and stopped at the Fishing Temple. Here there was a large barge and everyone went on board and fished, while a band played in another!

It was noticed that Victoria had winning ways:

> One day during the visit the King entered the drawing-room, leading his niece by the hand. 'Now, Victoria,' said His Majesty, 'the band is in the next room and shall play any tune you please. What shall it be?' The quick-witted Princess instantly replied, 'Oh, Uncle King, I should like *God Save the King*'. At the end of her visit he asked her what she had enjoyed most during her stay at Windsor. 'The drive I took with you, Uncle King,' was the answer.

George IV died when she was eleven. William IV and Queen Adelaide then presided over a rather more respectable Court. Greatly to William's annoyance, however, the Duchess of Kent continued to keep her daughter away. Instead, when the Princess was thirteen, the Duchess enraged the King by starting on a series of what he called 'royal progresses'. These were prolonged trips around the country designed to give the girl a better idea of the nation she would one day be called on to reign over. She stayed at the great country houses of the aristocracy. Henry Greville, who met her at Chatsworth, for instance, pronounced her 'gay and intelligent . . . both childlike and royal'.

Public occasions and the long journeys by coach were the parts of the 'progresses' she disliked most. At other times her girlish high spirits would bubble up. She loved riding and during a visit to North Wales she managed to do some galloping. 'Rosa went at an enormous rate; and literally *flew*.' 'Alas,' she added with a first glimpse of that nostalgia for which she was afterwards famous, 'it was our last ride at *dear* Plas Newydd.' When she arrived at Lord Fitzwilliam's estate at Wentworth Woodhouse she was soon observed running about in the garden.

> One wet morning, soon after her arrival, she was thus dis-porting herself, flitting from point to point, light-hearted and light-footed, when an old gardener, who did not then know her, seeing her about to descend a treacherous bit of ground from the terrace, called out, 'Be careful, Miss, it's slape!'—a Yorkshire word meaning slippery.
>
> The incautious, but ever-curious Princess, turning her head, asked 'What's slape?' and the same instant her feet flew from under her and she came down. The old gardener ran to lift her, saying, as he did so, '*That's slape, Miss*'.

At Burleigh, revealing her taste for slapstick, she could not contain her laughter when an extremely flustered waiter tipped a bucket of ice into her mother's lap. It was also with some relish that she recorded the Duchess's discomfort during a stormy boat trip: 'Mamma began to look queerish, but I thought it very pleasant.'

As the girl advanced into adolescence the behaviour of small children came increasingly to fascinate her. When her half sister Feodore brought over her two young children from Germany Victoria was in raptures. 'They are the dearest little loves I ever saw. . . . They were very funny and amusing and talked immensely.' To animals also, whether dogs, horses or birds, she was beginning a lifetime of devotion. Her first dog was a King Charles spaniel, 'dear sweet little Dash'. 'Little Dash is perfection,' she enthused, 'a darling.' He maintained his popularity after she became Queen, with the Prime Minister, Lord Melbourne, becoming one of his admirers.

Although visits to King William's Court were rare the Princess enjoyed herself when allowed to go. There was even the occasional Court Ball she was allowed to attend, enabling her to discover that her passion for the opera was matched by a passion for dancing. 'As you may understand,' she confirmed to her Uncle Leopold, 'my Operatic and Terpsichorean feelings are pretty strong.' When she was let out of her cage on the occasion of her fourteenth birthday her enthusiasm spilled over into the Journal she was now keeping.

> At half past seven we went to a Juvenile Ball that was given in my honour at St. James's by the King and Queen. We went into the Closet. Soon after the doors were opened and the King leading me went into the ball-room. Madame Bourdin was there as dancing-mistress . . . Dancing began soon after . . . I danced in all eight quadrilles. We came home at half past twelve. I was VERY much amused. . . .

The only limit, she found, to indulging her 'terpsichorean feelings' to the full was that 'in my station I unfortunately cannot valse or gallop'.

Another outing with the Royal Family was to Ascot Races. Here an American visitor noticed how simple were the young girl's tastes. 'The Queen and the young Princess Victoria,' he recorded, 'were leaning over a railing listening to a ballad singer, and seeming as much interested and amused as any simple country folk could be.' The Princess's own comment confirms her pleasure: 'I was very much amused indeed at the races.' She had, however, an additional reason for being pleased: she had had a bet with her Uncle William and won.

Anything unusual seemed to please her. Though ordinarily she did not care much for lessons, a lecture on physics 'illustrated by very curious and interesting experiments' found her 'very much amused'. Sermons always interested her. Also she had firm opinions about music, having little time, for instance, for 'old tiresome Handel'. Her tastes were modern. 'I like the present Italian school such as Rossini, Bellini, Donizetti & C. much better.' When she later told Lord Melbourne that she considered Mozart old-fashioned 'he clasped his hands and looked up in astonishment'.

The musical tastes of the Princess were commendably indulged by her mother. As a sixteenth birthday treat the Duchess arranged a special concert. Victoria was 'most exceedingly delighted—it was a most delicious concert—I shall never forget it'. A typical entry in her Journal shows how much her attention was also captured by her visits to the opera.

> We came in just at the beginning of the Opera of *Anna Boulena* . . . Mdlle Guiletta Grisi . . . is a most beautiful singer and actress and is likewise very young and pretty. She sang *beautifully* throughout . . . but particularly in the last act when she is mad, when she *acted* likewise *beautifully*. . . . We came up at twelve. I was VERY MUCH AMUSED INDEED.

Occasionally she was taken to a play. She was 'VERY MUCH AMUSED' at seeing Macready in *King John*. *The Innkeeper's Daughter* she thought 'very horrible but *extremely interesting*'. Her theatrical experience varied from *Macbeth* and *Hamlet* to 'the pantomime which is called *Old Mother Hubbard and Her Dog*'. Not unnaturally for someone of her age she preferred the light to the heavy, but irrespective of what she was watching she was fascinated by the appearance and idiosyncracies of those she saw on the stage. Thus, in *Cenerentola*, she thought 'the sisters were two

FRIGHTENING creatures'. But when Taglioni danced she 'looked *lovely* for she is all-ways smiling'.

When the Duchess arranged for her daughter to be taught singing by the famous Italian singer Lablache, the Princess thought it 'delightful'. 'I like Lablache very much, he is such a nice good-natured, good-humoured man, and a very patient and excellent master; and he is very merry too'. His appearance did not escape the microscope of the royal eyes. 'It amused me always to see him come in and out of my room; he walked so erect and made such a fine dignified bow.' She wished that he taught her every day instead of once a week. His lessons in fact were such a joy that she kept them going long after she became Queen.

By the time the Princess was sixteen she discovered she was fond of the company of young men, especially handsome, jolly young men. A combination of 'beauty' and 'mirth' she found irresistible. She was delighted at this time to receive a visit from two German cousins from Coburg, Ferdinand and Augustus. 'They are both very handsome and dear,' she enthused. What is more, they were 'most funny and childishly merry, which I delight in.' A few months later two more Coburg cousins arrived. Their names were Ernest and Albert. This visit gave her even more pleasure. 'Dearly as I love Ferdinand, and also good Augustus,' she was soon writing, 'I love Ernest and Albert *more* than them, oh yes, M UCH more.' 'Albert, who is just as tall as Ernest but stouter, is extremely handsome,' she decided, 'but the charm of his countenance is his expression, which is most delightful.' Above all, she liked them both because they were both 'so merry'. 'They like very much talking about serious and instructive things and yet are so *very very* merry and gay and happy, like young people ought to be.'

The round of merry dinners, dances and party games which these cousins' visits brought with them opened up a window on a new and appealing world for a girl now longing to stretch her wings. Above all the visits highlighted her desire for 'gaiety' and 'mirth', and her natural inclination to be merry—'just as young people ought to be'. For a short while they pushed aside the walls

1 Princess Victoria aged ten. 'An affectionate and high-spirited child.'

2 Aged eleven. Now heiress-presumptive to the throne

3 Victoria aged seventeen. 'All this dissipation does me good.'

4 The young Queen. 'She has great animal spirits.'

of her prison-like existence and relieved the tyranny her elders were imposing on her. 'I can assure you,' she told her Uncle Leopold, 'all this dissipation does me a great deal of good.'

Luckily for her, the time was fast approaching when her taste for 'dissipation' could be indulged to the full.

CHAPTER II

Merry Monarch

A month after Princess Victoria's eighteenth birthday King William died and the doors of her prison sprang open. No new monarch emerging into the world has been greeted with more intense public interest. Not only is a female Sovereign unusual, but no one as young had succeeded to the throne for nearly three hundred years. She herself felt it was all 'like a dream'. Nevertheless she took to the throne like a duck to water. 'I delight in this work . . . I really have an immense amount to do; I receive so many communications from my Ministers but I like it very much.' Even so, her duties took her aback sometimes. 'I had my hand kissed nearly *3000* times!'

Her natural dignity, in spite of a diminutive figure, made a great impression. From the great Duke of Wellington downwards the Privy Councillors at her Accession Council were amazed at her self-possession. Her kind treatment of her infirm uncle, the Duke of Sussex, showed that she had a heart, though another incident was reported which showed that behind the kindness lay strength of character:

> When she had occasion to recapitulate the title of an old Act of Parliament in which the word 'intitulated' was used instead of 'entitled', Lord Melbourne, standing by her side, said, 'entitled, please, Your Majesty'. She turned quickly towards him with a look of surprise, and looking again at the paper repeated in a louder voice, 'An Act intitulated'.

The Bishop of London's comments summed up the impressions

of those who observed her during these early days. 'When the Bishops were first presented to the Queen,' he said, 'she received them with all possible dignity and then retired. She passed through a glass door and forgetting its transparency, was seen to run off like the girl she is.'

When it came to moving from Kensington to the newly-completed Buckingham Palace feelings of nostalgia swept over her. In spite of some unhappy memories she was, as she said, 'fond of the poor old Palace'. But once the move was made she was more than satisfied. As she told the young Marchioness of Salisbury, 'the view was so much gayer, and she could see from her dressing room the people walking and driving in the park—that she was delighted with London . . . She preferred driving in the streets, she told me, infinitely to driving out of town—the Regent's Park was quite country enough'. 'She has no affectation of being older than she is,' Lady Salisbury concluded, but was possessed of 'a great turn for seizing the ridiculous. If any fault could be found it might be that she laughs a little too much.' David Wilkie, who painted the picture of her Accession Council, got a similar impression. 'She had all the decision, thought, and self-possession of a queen of older years; has all the buoyancy of youth, and from her smile to the unrestrained laughter is a perfect child.'

The inveterate gossip and letter-writer, Creevey, was fascinated by the account he had from Lady Cowley: 'The Queen,' she said, 'was excessively civil to everyone, had excellent manners, but was *Royal* (and quite right, little Vic, say I); and Lady Cowley adds that in the evening the Queen relaxed, and nothing could be more amiable or agreeable than she was'. 'Could you wish,' old Creevey asked, 'for a better account of a little tit of eighteen made all at once into a Queen?' A little later he went to Court himself and was able to confirm this impression:

She was told by Lord Conyngham that I had not been presented, upon which a scene took place that to me was truly distressing. The poor little thing could not get her glove off. I never was so annoyed in my whole life; yet what could I do? But she blushed and laughed and pulled, till the thing was done, and I kissed her hand . . .

A more homely little thing you never beheld, *when she is at her ease,* and she is evidently dying to be more so. She laughs in real earnest, opening her mouth as wide as it can go, showing not very pretty gums . . . She blushes and laughs every instant in so natural a way as to disarm anybody.

'She has,' agreed Charles Greville, Clerk of the Privy Council, 'great animal spirits and enters into the magnificent novelties of her position with the zest and curiosity of a child.' 'Her laugh is to me particularly delightful,' echoed Mrs. Stevenson, the American Minister's wife, 'it is so full of girlish glee and gladness, whilst her countenance beams with such an expression of innocence and sweetness . . .'

During the early months of the reign, because of Court mourning for the late King, organised amusements had to be avoided. Meanwhile, though, she was able, for the first time, to enjoy reading as many novels as she wished. She tried Dickens' *Oliver Twist* 'which I must say is excessively interesting'. Bulwer Lytton's *Eugene Aram* she thought 'fearfully interesting'. Still, she was glad when she had finished it, 'for I never feel quite at ease or at home when I am reading a novel'. Considering her narrow upbringing it is small wonder that she still had a conscience on the subject. Nevertheless, the taste for novels, once acquired, was never lost. She continued to find them 'fearfully interesting' and read them with girlish gusto all her life.

Her enjoyment of riding was equally intense. Her Journal became full of horses. 'I have got two such *darlings*, if I may use that word.' She did not spare them. On a long ride to Richmond 'we rode very hard and Tartar MOST delightfully, NEVER was there SUCH a dear horse'. Another day she ventured 'a good way on the Harrow Road, I should say within four or five miles of Harrow—then down a pretty narrow lane where one could fancy oneself two or three hundred miles from London, out by Willesden Field (where I had never been) and Kilburn'. Once her

horse shied 'and I came off . . . not a bit hurt or put out or frightened, but astonished and amused'. Her Aunt Louise was not so
lucky. Her horse was frightened by thunder and '*ran away, full
gallop*, to our great horror, and poor Aunt Louise lost her hat'.

In the evenings she enjoyed such dissipations as games of Tactics
and Fox and Geese. Certainly things had come a long way since
the Regent's day. Even games of draughts were such a novel
experience for her that more worldly onlookers found themselves
getting caught up in the excitement. 'I got so interested,' confessed
Charles Murray, 'that when Her Majesty made one very bad
move I groaned audibly: she looked over her shoulder and
laughed very much when she saw me.' In spite of the advice of
attendant ministers she was equally unsuccessful when she and her
Aunt Louise tried their hand at chess. 'All gave me advice, and all
different advice . . . and *all* got so *eager* that it was very amusing.'
It was not, as she drily noted, a good recommendation for Cabinet
government: 'Between them all I got quite beat, and Aunt Louise
triumphed over my Council of Ministers.'

Sometimes there was a little improvised singing. Victoria
herself had a good clear voice, but was nervous singing in public.
She found a kindred spirit in Georgiana Liddell, one of the young
Maids of Honour:

> One day the Queen expressed a desire to hear me sing, so in
> fear and trembling I sang one of Grisi's famous airs, but omitted
> a shake at the end. The Queen's quick ear immediately detected
> the omission, and smiling Her Majesty said, 'Does not your
> sister shake, Lady Normanby?' My sister immediately ans-
> wered, 'Oh yes, Ma'am, she is shaking all over.' The Queen,
> much amused, laughed heartily at the joke.

Once Court mourning was out of the way she was able to
indulge in her love of dancing. It now developed into an absolute
passion—partly, no doubt, because it provided her with some of
her few opportunities to let herself go. The first State Ball of her
reign gave a foretaste of joys to come.

> I never heard anything as *beautiful* in my life as Strauss's band . . .

I did not leave the ball-room till 10 m. to *four*! and I was in bed by ½ p. 4—the sun shining. It was a lovely ball, so gay, so nice—and I felt so happy and merry . . .

'Dear little thing,' wrote the American Minister's wife, 'she danced with all her heart, and said the next day she was "so happy".' Her older attendants were less enthusiastic—'Poor Lady Lansdowne, who is in waiting, said she was "half-dead" '.

Regular dancing now became a permanent feature of Court life. Georgiana Liddell was to have nostalgic memories of how at Buckingham Palace 'one lovely summer's morning we had danced till dawn, and the quadrangle then being open to the east, Her Majesty went on to the roof of the portico to see the sun rise'. 'We kept the dancing up till past three,' Victoria herself told Melbourne, 'and the Queen was much amused, and slept soundly till half-past ten, which she is much ashamed of'. During a visit to London by the Hereditary Grand-Duke of Russia—the Czarevitch —some unusual dances were added to the royal repertoire. All were lovingly described in the Queen's Journal.

After supper they danced a Mazurka for ½ an hour, I should think nearly; the Grand-Duke asked me to take a turn, which I did (never having done it before) and which is very pleasant . . . After this we danced (which I had never seen before) the 'Grossvater' or 'Rerraut', which is excessively amusing. I danced with the Grand-Duke, and we had much fun and laughter . . . It begins with a solemn walk round the room; which also follows each figure; one figure, in which a lady and gentleman run holding their pocket-handkerchief by each end, and letting the ladies on one side of it go under it, and the gentlemen jump over it, is too funny . . . I never enjoyed myself more. We were all so merry.

Another indulgence was the London theatre. In this Melbourne encouraged her. 'Talked of my going to the Play in State again, and Lord M. said, "If you like it, it's a popular thing".' Macready, at Covent Garden, thought her theatrical tastes too light. If they were light nothing would have been more natural in a girl still in her teens. Yet really he had little cause for complaint, for in addition to enjoying farces she took in *King Lear* and *The Tempest*. Certainly no one could criticise her enthusiasm for grand opera. 'It was the new opera *Lucrezia Borgia* by Donizetti,' runs a typical entry in her Journal, 'the music is very beautiful, and the story a dreadful tragedy. Grisi looked beautiful; and sang and acted superbly. . . .' Another time, 'it was again *Norma*, and oh! more splendid than before. . . . Grisi was perfection; it was quite a treat to hear her. Mario too was delightful . . .'

More often, though, the royal taste was less sophisticated and the child could be seen peeping out from behind the monarch. When Van Amburgh brought his lions to Drury Lane one visit was not enough. With no more thought than a small child would have for the caged existence of the animals she went eagerly to see them six times in as many weeks. It was when she was able to relax like this that she enjoyed being young. Her desire to unbend and be natural at home too accentuated her old love of animals. Melbourne told her she would be smothered by all the dogs she acquired, and was horrified when she told him she would like a monkey.

Partly for the same reason, and partly because of her maternal instinct, children were also assured of a warm welcome. 'The Queen will be delighted to see Lady John Russell's little girl,' runs one of her letters, 'and would be very happy if Lady John would bring the *Baby* also.' Lady Sandwich was actually appointed to the Royal Household when she was pregnant. Afterwards she was encouraged to have her baby with her when she was in waiting. Little ceremony was observed on such occasions. 'Directly I arrived the Queen came up, and finding him on the floor, she was on all-fours with him during her visit.' To have older children playing in her room was a great delight. Then she could indulge in her love of romping. 'After dinner,' one of her Ministers noted, 'two young children, sons of Princess Leiningen, who was at table, came into the room and romped and played about, and kissed the Queen's hands, and she kissed them and laughed heartily at their little sports and encouraged them.'

Children, like animals, are good judges of human kindness. Throughout Queen Victoria's life children responded to her approaches and were at ease with her. How this delighted her is shown in her reaction to a visit by Lord Conyngham's children, aged seven and five. 'They would hardly let me go,' she crooned. 'They are charming, delightful children, quite at home with me and treat me quite like a playfellow, which pleased me much.'

Among the adult members of the Queen's Household her amiability inspired similar devotion. Her tolerant, easy-going ways (sometimes taken advantage of) come across clearly in Creevey's story of a new lady-in-waiting arriving at Windsor Castle, and immediately filling her apron with books from the library.

> Passing thro' the gallery in this state, whom should she meet but little Vic! Great was her perturbation, for in the first place a low curtsey was necessary, and what was to come of the books, for they must curtsey too. Then to be found with all this property within the first half hour of her coming, and before even she had seen Vic! . . . But Vic was much amused with the thing altogether, and laughed heartily and was as good humoured as ever she could be.

At the prorogation of Parliament it was Lady Lyttelton's turn to appreciate this good humour:

> My duties turned out unexpectedly important and arduous and frightened me much. After the Duchess of Sutherland had changed Her Majesty's robe, with the help of the dressers, I had . . . in the presence of the whole Court, and surrounded by the great officers of State, to unpin and remove from Her Majesty's head her diamond diadem, and taking the great Crown of England (weighing 12 pounds) from some grandee . . . to place it and *pin it on* with two diamond pins through the velvet and her hair on the back of her head! Feel for me!
>
> All this I did however pretty well. But when I had to do it all over again on Her Majesty's return, she was in a hurry, and the *last* pin I *could* not find the proper place for in the diadem,

and first ran it against the royal head (upon which she looked up with a comical arch look of entreaty), and then could not put it in at all anywhere . . .

It has furnished a most invaluable story against me to Her Majesty, and two good *bon mots*. On returning to the palace, of course I made an immediate confession to Mme. de Lehzen. She answered, 'Oh, do not mind! Do not *care a pin for de pin*. All deed so well, it does not matter at all!' And at dinner when the Queen told Lord Melbourne the story, saying, 'To be sure, it was very nervous for poor Lady L. to do so before so many people all looking at her, and never having done such a thing before,' Lord Melbourne most wittily answered: 'Your Majesty might have said as Mary Queen of Scots did on the scaffold, "*I am not accustomed to be undressed before so many people, nor by such attendants!*" ' Wasn't it very clever? Such a perfectly apposite quotation, and so comically applied. Mary Stuart of course you will remember was disrobed by her executioners.

This was only one occasion among many that Lord Melbourne's clever, apposite remarks added spice to the life of the young Queen. Indeed it was in the company of her Prime Minister that Victoria spent some of her happiest hours. From the outset their association was important to both of them. To Melbourne it gave both the female company for which his nature craved, and scope for his paternal feelings. As Greville succinctly put it: 'He is a man with an infinite capacity for loving without having anything in the world to love.' On the other side, Greville was convinced that the Queen's feelings were 'sexual though she does not know it'. Here he was wrong. Melbourne for her was a father-figure, something she was to spend most of life looking for. 'He explained it like a kind father would do to his child,' she would write; 'he has something so fatherly and so affectionate and so kind in him, that one must love him.'

Even more important, as she quickly discovered, Melbourne was 'merry', 'amusing', and 'amazingly funny'. His diverting comments, on even the most ordinary subjects, found their way into the Queen's Journal.

Lord Melbourne was very funny about the caps and bonnets; he looked round the table and said, 'There is an amazing cargo of bonnets and things come from Paris I fancy,' which made us laugh . . . Spoke of clothes about which Lord M. was very funny; said the fewer you have the better, and he was certain it was very bad to keep things in *store*, at which we laughed much, and said it would be impossible for ladies to keep dresses in store, as fashions always changed. . . . Lord M. said he was quite well, and when I said I thought him not well the night before, he said, 'Only sleepy; that is not a sign of being ill; it's right to sleep after dinner; we all ought to lie down all round the room and sleep,' which made me laugh very much.

Even on more serious topics Lord Melbourne's distilled wisdom was so down-to-earth, so pithily expressed as to provoke mirth. On historical matters his views were often highly unorthodox and loud laughter usually resulted.

Talked of Henry VIII. Lord M. said, 'Those women bothered him so.' . . . poor Katharine of Aragon he ill-used, I said; 'He got tired of her', said Lord M., 'she was a sad, groaning, moaning woman,' which made us all laugh.

Although leader of a Whig administration Melbourne was not in the least progressive. A great deal of his philosophy can be discerned from his opinion of the recently published *Oliver Twist*.

. . . he read half of the first volume at Panshanger. 'It's all among Workhouses, and Coffin Makers, and Pickpockets,' he said, 'I don't like that low debasing view of mankind. . . . Schiller and Goethe would have been shocked at such things.' Lehzen said they would not have disliked reading them. 'She don't know her literature,' said Lord M. . . . He kept us in fits of laughter by all this—as also in talking of Lady Bulwer's book, he said, 'I daresay she has been a scribbling woman all her life.'

Another literary discussion revealed his aristocratic reservations about the up-and-coming middle classes.

Talked of a novel by Miss Martineau called *Deerbrook*, which Lady Lyttelton was praising very much, and which she said was about the Middle Classes. 'I don't like the Middle Classes,' Lord M. said. . . . I said to Lord M. he so often kept me in hot water by saying *such* things before, and to, people; 'It's a good thing to surprise,' he said. I said he said such things of people's families to them. 'That's a very good thing,' he replied funnily, 'I do that on purpose, I think it right to warn people of the faults of their families'; and he turned to [the third baron] Lilford and said, 'Your family has always been reckoned very prosing, so I warn you of that,' which made us laugh so.

He poked fun at other aristocrats. Lord Tavistock, he thought, had 'some strange notions', but then 'he lives a great deal in the country, and people who live a great deal in the country pick up strange ideas'.

It is not surprising that a man with Melbourne's scepticism should have had reservations about the Church and conventional religion. 'Talked of the Archbishop of York and his being so wonderful for his age,' wrote the Queen, 'I made Lord Melbourne laugh by saying he told me that Lord M. had said to him, "You bishops are sad dogs".' In her dry way she was also able to make him laugh over his erratic attendance at church.

Talked of Anderson's preaching; and Lord M. said, 'I'm afraid to go to church for fear of hearing something very extraordinary'. I laughed and said he never went, and that he always managed very conveniently to be either unable to come down for a Sunday, or too ill, which made him laugh very much.

It was during a discussion on preachers that Melbourne came out with one of his most typical *bon mots*. 'I observed to Lord Melbourne that there were not very many good preachers to be found; he replied in the affirmative and added, "But there are not *very many good* anything".' He spoke in a similar vein when the Duke of Richmond lamented that many people came out of

prison worse than they went in. 'I am afraid,' said the Prime
Minister, 'there are many places one comes out of worse than one
went in; one often comes out worse of a ballroom than one went
in.' The same light-hearted cynicism came out when the Queen
made a fuss of a strange dog. 'Dogs get so familiar,' commented
Melbourne, 'that they behave as well as any man—*better* than
some.' His views on hypnotism (called magnetism in those days)
have the same ring. 'I said it was very disagreeable to be magnetised, as people got to say such odd things in this magnetic state.
"Why," said Lord Melbourne, "people say odd enough things
without being magnetised".'

Sometimes it was the Queen's self-deprecating observations
that amused Melbourne. When Baron Munchausen was presented
as the new Hanoverian Minister, 'I told Lord M. of my last recollection of Baron Munchausen, namely, my giving him a
commission to send me some wax dolls from Berlin, which made
Lord Melbourne laugh excessively'. There was a typical bit of
repartee when the Queen, being fond of both food and ale, discovered she was putting on weight—'To my horror weigh 8 stone
13!!' People should only eat when they are hungry, suggested Melbourne. 'In that case,' came her reply, 'I should be eating all day.'

In spite of her sheltered upbringing Queen Victoria had enough
Hanoverian blood in her to respond to Melbourne's more earthy
anecdotes.

> The Duke of Orleans was a violent man, Lord M. continued,
> and he showed the Duke of Burgundy into a room full of pic-
> tures, 'and he said to the Duke, "All these ladies have been my
> mistresses," and the the first was the Duchess of Burgundy.'

She loved a story with a clever twist to it:

> Lord Melbourne . . . told me of an affront which the 'Dema-
> gogue Hunt' offered William Peel one day, in the House of
> Commons, on the latter's attacking him. William Peel said
> something derogatory about Hunt's extraction, upon which
> Hunt replied: 'If *my* father was the *first gentleman* of his family,
> *your* father was the *last gentleman* of *his* family.'

Lord Melbourne said . . . that the present Lord Bessborough's father lived to be a very great age; Lord Melbourne said he was the man of whom the following anecdote is told: he (*that* Lord Bessborough) was playing at cards, at Picquet, Lord Melbourne thinks, when his partner dropped down dead; and he said to the Waiter, 'Remember, if the gentleman recovers, that I've got such and such a thing in my hand . . .'

Since girlhood she had had a taste for stories of this kind. Now she built up quite a collection. She passed one on to her Uncle Leopold when Talleyrand died: 'Did you know what Pozzo said to someone about him? He said he (Talleyrand) would not die yet, "*parce que le diable ne voulait pas l'avoir*".' Talleyrand was just the sort of man to fascinate her. He appealed to her taste for the unusual, the bizarre, the *outré*. It is this taste which explains her intense interest in Melbourne's stories about George IV and Queen Caroline. His account of the divorce proceedings she found especially diverting—'"Lord Egremont said," continued Lord Melbourne, "As for Guilford, he twaddled like a waiting maid when he gave evidence; but his sister lied like a man".'

Melbourne himself of course had a touch of the bizarre about him. This was part of his appeal. She hoped that their close association would last for ever. It lasted four years till Melbourne's resignation the year after her marriage. Later she was to look back on these years as constituting the most frivolous chapter in her life. No doubt they did, and it was only natural that they should. After a secluded childhood and suppressed adolescence she had come to the throne when she was old enough to spread her wings and young enough to enjoy herself. Nevertheless her pleasures remained simple, and though she was frivolous sometimes she did not become blasé. Marriage was certainly to add an extra dimension to her happiness but it was based on simple tastes which, like her character, were established before she met Albert. In particular her wish to be amused was there in strong measure when she married and it was never afterwards to desert her for long.

CHAPTER III

Dearest Albert

As Queen Victoria well knew, it had long been the wish of her mother's family that she would one day marry her cousin Albert. His visit to England when they were seventeen had left happy memories. After her birdcage-upbringing, however, she found her freedom as an unmarried queen had its attractions. As she confided to Lord Melbourne, 'I dreaded the thought of marrying; that I was so accustomed to have my own way, that I thought it was 10 to 1 that I shouldn't agree with any one'. It was therefore with mixed feelings that she agreed to another visit by Albert. They were now both twenty. What she wanted was a love match. She tried to make it clear in advance that she would not have him if she found she did not care for him. Once she saw him however everything changed. 'It was with some emotion that I beheld Albert—who is *beautiful*.' His previous boyish good looks had now developed into the type of manly beauty that fascinated her.

He and his brother arrived before their luggage. They appeared at Court the first evening, as Victoria quaintly put it, 'in spite of their morning dresses'. 'Having no clothes they could not appear at dinner, but nevertheless *débuted* after dinner in their *negligé*. Ernest is grown quite handsome; Albert's *beauty* is most *striking*, and he is so amiable and unaffected—in short, very fascinating.' His dancing had improved along with his appearance. 'It is quite a pleasure to look at Albert when he gallops and valses, he does it so beautifully, holds himself so well with that beautiful figure of his.'

She was equally pleased to discover that he was still as easily amused by harmless pastimes as she was. 'I played 2 games of

Tactics with dearest Albert, and 2 of Fox and Geese. Stayed up till 20 m. p. 11, a delightful evening.' Like her, he could laugh loudly at Lord Melbourne's cynicism.

I sat on the sofa with Albert and we played at the game of letters, out of which you have to make words, and we had great fun with them. Albert gave 'Pleasure', and when I said to the people who were puzzling it out, it was a very common word, Albert said, But not a very common *thing*, upon which Lord M. said, 'It is truth, or honesty?' which made us all laugh.

It was to father-figure Melbourne that the Queen first confided her rapid change of mind about marrying. In doing so she did not fail to see the funny side of the predicament in which her regal status placed her.

After a little pause I said to Lord M. . . . that I had made up my mind (about marrying dearest Albert) . . . Then I asked, if I hadn't better tell Albert of my decision soon, in which Lord M. agreed. How? I asked, for that in general such things were done the other way,—which made Lord M. laugh.

Shortly afterwards she arranged a tête-á-tête with 'dearest Albert', and it is clear she managed the delicate situation beautifully.

I said to him . . . that it would made me *too happy* if he would consent to what I wished (to marry me). We embraced each other, and he was *so* kind, *so* affectionate. I said I was quite unworthy of him,—he said he would be very happy 'das Leben mit dir zu zubringen,' and was so kind, and seemed so happy, that I really felt it was the happiest brightest moment of my life.

Albert was genuinely touched by her humility, and by her saying that it would be a 'sacrifice' for him to marry her. 'The joyous openness with which she told me this enchanted me, and I was quite carried away by it.' Later there was a new experience which Victoria greatly enjoyed—'We kissed each other again and again.' As Queen there was no Victorian chaperone constantly in attendance on *her*.

The wedding was fixed for three months later. (Even Lord Melbourne took pains over the preparations. 'Lord M. made us laugh excessively about his new coat, which he said, "I expect it to be the thing most observed".') According to an American account of the ceremony, 'the only comic part of the whole affair was when the poor German prince "endowed her with all his worldly goods"'. Afterwards there was a brief honeymoon at Windsor. The first evening, the Queen recorded, Albert's 'excessive love and affection gave me feelings of heavenly love and happiness'. Albert in a black velvet jacket open at the neck she thought 'more beautiful than it is possible for me to say'. Still, they were out walking very early next morning, which, lamented Greville, was 'not the way to provide us with a Prince of Wales'. The next evening they gave a merry dinner party, and the evening after there was a dance—something which shocked the more conventional. Perhaps the knowledge that Albert had helped her put on her stockings would have shocked them even more.

Lady Lyttelton realised the full significance of the Queen's change of status. She knew that, for all Victoria's affability, it was 'a new thing for her to *dare* to be *unguarded* in conversation with anybody; and with her frank and fearless nature the restraints she has hitherto been under from one reason or another must have been most painful'. Matrimony was in fact both a safety valve and a safe haven for Queen Victoria. There was the occasional letting off of steam; more often there was the calm feeling of security.

Albert was something of an enigma. One commonly held view was that he was exceedingly 'Germanic', i.e. humourless and heavy. Under his guidance, it has been suggested, his wife changed from a high-spirited girl into a colourless, dependant creature whose opinions were a carbon copy of his own. This, however, was far from being the case. For one thing, the Prince was not nearly as devoid of humour as outsiders were inclined to assume. 'He is full of talent and fun,' was how his match-making Uncle Leopold had commended him. Victoria herself, in making up her mind to marry him, had been quick to spot his good nature, his sense of humour and his capacity for being easily amused.

5 Her etching of Albert at the time of their marriage. 'The type of manly beauty that fascinated her.'

Queen Victoria the year after her marriage. 'We have been *very* gay.'

7 The Queen's etching of
the baby Princess Royal,
with nurse and parrot

8 A nude study by Queen Victoria done from
a photograph in 1860. She and Albert used to
exchange nude pictures

Nor did marriage change Queen Victoria as much as has some-times been imagined. She herself was to foster the belief that after her marriage 'all changed'. In reality, the change was neither as sudden or as all-embracing as this might lead one to suppose. Though they were an utterly devoted couple, and though she came to depend on him to a tremendous degree, it was her grief after his death that resulted in her projecting him as absolute per-fection. Letters she wrote during his lifetime cast a rather different light on her feelings. She 'grieved,' for instance, after twelve years of marriage that 'Albert becomes really a *terrible* man of business; I think it takes a little from the gentleness of his character, and makes him preoccupied'. Political worries she considered he took 'too much to heart'. 'He is often very trying in his hastiness and over-love of business.' In consequence his constitution became undermined and he upset what she was pleased to call 'his poor dear stomach'. True, these were small clouds in an otherwise cloudless sky, but the fact that the Queen herself pointed to them proves that even in the later stages of married life she was not the all-adoring, submissive creature that has sometimes been imagined. Much as she might depend on her husband's judgement, she was not under his thumb.

Prince Albert of course had his difficulties in adapting himself to marriage with the monarch of a strange country. His own manner did not help. When he was not at ease among friends his behaviour could appear stiff. In the right circumstances he could be very good company. 'The fun that was latent in Prince Albert's nature made his society most amusing to his companions,' a Scottish duke remembered, 'for he was an excellent mimic, and used to take off the professors at College.' 'He had little small talk,' commented another Scottish observer, 'but I have seen him con-verse with great eagerness and animation, and his face light up with keen interest and often with quiet humour when discussing a congenial topic.' Like his wife he tended to be more at ease with servants than in society. Many years after his death one of the old servants at Balmoral vividly remembered his 'kindness of heart and his invariable good-humour; met you always with a smile;

if your work pleased him he said so, and if it did not he said so; but always with the same kind smile'. Within the family circle the smile was much in evidence. The Queen, who before their marriage had so admired 'that dear sunny face', after living with him over twenty years was to remember 'that bright loving smile with which he ever greeted her'.

Certainly high spirits were often in evidence during the early days of married life. 'Frequently during the evening they conversed,' reported the American Minister's wife, 'and several times laughed with merry glee at the communications they made to each other.' A book of caricatures would keep him happy all evening. 'The Prince showed us all of them last evening,' runs one of Lady Lyttelton's letters, 'running from one to the other laughing so loud himself as to be quite noisy and boyish.' He was not above playing blind man's buff with the ladies, and on occasion would slip out of the dining room before the other men in order to play duets with the Queen. Georgiana Liddell thought he and the Queen well matched in their simple tastes.

> We had such a gay evening last night, for after dinner the Queen began polkaing with Countess Wratislaw, and made her give a regular dancing lesson. We afterwards played a new German game, and then another of my accomplishments was brought into play, for the Prince began spinning counters, so I took to spinning rings, which you know I am adept at doing, and the Queen was delighted.
>
> It always entertains me to see the little things which amuse Her Majesty and the Prince, instead of their looking bored as peoples so often do in English Society.

Eleanor Stanley found that the Prince's appreciation of a funny story was also as keen as his wife's: 'The Prince told good stories very well indeed and was the first to laugh at them himself.' As Queen Victoria herself confirmed, within the bosom of his family this side of the Prince was much to the fore. 'At breakfast and luncheon and also at family dinners', she later recorded, 'he sat at the top of the table, and kept us all enlivened by his interesting conversation, by his charming anecdotes and droll stories without end of his childhood, of people at Coburg, of our good people in Scotland and endless amusing stories he would repeat with a wonderful power of mimicry, and at which he would himself laugh most heartily.' Georgiana Liddell collected two examples of the simple stories that appear to have appealed to him most.

One was that the mother of a girl going into service in a Duke's establishment gave her daughter strict instructions to say 'Your Grace', if ever the Duke spoke to her. The girl promised to pay attention to this, and departed. A few days afterwards the Duke met her in a passage and asked her some questions, which instead of answering, the poor girl immediately began, 'For what I have received,' etc.

On another occasion, an Inspector was examining children at the Duke's school. Among the questions he asked the meaning of the word 'grace', upon which the children all exclaimed with one accord that it meant the Duke of Rutland!

Another favourite of Albert's was the story of the fat lady of Coburg who dressed up for dinner in a white frock. A short-sighted man mistook her for a porcelain stove and, parting his coat-tails, turned his back on her to warm himself.

In early married life one of the Prince's greatest trials was a chronic inability to stay awake late at night. Lord Melbourne rather envied him—'I am very glad to hear it'—but at a Palace concert Guizot, the French ambassador, noticed the embarrass-ment the weakness could cause.

The Queen took a more lively interest in it than the greater part of her guests did. Prince Albert slept. She looked at him, half-smiling, half-vexed. She pushed him with her elbow. He woke up, and nodded approval of the piece of the moment. Then he went to sleep again, still nodding approval, and the Queen began again.

'The Queen was charmed,' another visitor noticed, 'and Cousin

Albert looked beautiful, and slept quietly as usual.' As in most marriages, a certain amount of adjustment was necessary before a *modus vivendi* was established. Over late nights a compromise appears to have been reached. Whereas Albert had been inclined to fall asleep at 9.30, and Victoria could cheerfully go on into the small hours, 11 o'clock became the accepted bed-time. The pleasures of the dance certainly continued. The Prince's accomplishments matched the Queen's natural flair and enthusiasm. Once they were engaged he had taught her to waltz, a new pleasure which etiquette had hitherto forbidden her to indulge in. After marriage, as before, every occasion was used as an excuse for dancing. 'The Queen spent a very merry, happy birthday at dear old Claremont,' she gaily wrote to Melbourne when she was twenty three, 'and we finished by dancing in the gallery.' On the Duchess of Kent's birthday there was another dance—'great fun, but rather a romp' according to Georgiana Liddell. 'We have been *very* gay,' the Queen told her Uncle Leopold at the beginning of 1843, 'danced into the New Year, and again last night, and were *very* merry, though but a small party.'

On a grander scale a series of fancy-dress balls was inaugurated at Buckingham Palace. At the first Victoria and Albert appeared as Queen Philippa and Edward III. It was such a brilliant and successful occasion that it was soon followed by a ball covering the reigns of George II and George III. Later there was a Stuart ball and 'a very grand *bal poudré* at which', it was reported, 'Her Majesty danced a Minuet with infinite grace'. Not that everyone was in favour of these grand affairs, though one reason for holding them was to create employment among the Spitalfields weavers. Sir John Hobhouse was one of those who did not quite approve. His first ball he called 'a childish frolic of H.M'. The costumes were so bizarre 'we all laughed at one another'. Still, he had to confess 'I waited to see the Sir Roger de Coverly in the long gallery, danced by a hundred and fifty couples I should think, H.M. leading.'

There were other occasions, too, when it was suggested that, far from being too staid, the royal couple were not staid enough.

Criticism of their excessive interest in animals, and the part this played in the emergence of matinée performances, finds its way into the history of entertainment. So keen was the Royal family on Astley's Circus and the American circus at the Alhambra that they arranged for private performances to take place during the day. These 'new-fangled daytime matinées' were widely condemned at the time as 'undesirable innovations'.

The American showman P. T. Barnum made his fortune in England out of the royal taste for freaks. He had come to London with a 25-inch-high midget, called General Tom Thumb, but made little headway till the Queen invited him to bring Tom Thumb to the Palace. Barnum later told his fellow-Americans of his protegé's instant success.

The general toddled in, looking like a wax-doll gifted with the power of locomotion. Surprise and pleasure were depicted on the countenance of the royal circle, at beholding this *mite* of humanity so much smaller than they had evidently expected to find him ... The Queen then took him by the hand, led him about the gallery, and asked him many questions the answers to which kept the party in an uninterrupted strain of merriment.

The visit was mentioned in the Court Circular, much to the disgust of *Punch*. Such was the 'General's' success that other visits followed. The Queen introduced her children: 'General, this is the Prince of Wales'—'How do you do, Prince'. She liked this carefree manner. When she asked for a song he suggested *Yankee Doodle Dandee*. Barnum was embarrassed because of its association with the War of Independence. He had no cause to worry. 'When the merriment it occasioned had somewhat subsided, the Queen good-humoredly remarked, "That is a very pretty song, General. Sing it if you please."'

The overall picture that emerges from these early years of married life is of Albert enjoying his moments of leisure and encouraging his wife in the harmless pleasures that appealed to her. She was, as he once boasted, 'the most perfect companion a man could wish to have'. A letter he wrote his brother after five years of marriage, just prior to their first visit to Coburg together, shows how much he considered her tastes.

> We by no means expect grand festivals. What I think would give Victoria a great deal of pleasure would be to see the children's festival and a dinner in the Anger would be something *perfectly new* and characteristic of Coburg. All the peasants from the country who come to Coburg on such occasions and their various costumes would interest Victoria.
>
> We shall probably go to the theatre several times and I would recommend characteristically German plays, Kotzebue, and German comedies and the Huguenottes. Victoria likes such things very much . . .

A husband could hardly have provided for his wife's entertainment with more forethought. Yet, ironically, her greatest pleasure during this visit was watching his excitement at being back home. Unhappily, on their return home she heard it said that she had not smiled enough. (She could take comfort: she was not to be the last royal personage at whom this accusation would be levelled.) Lady Lyttelton watched Albert's reaction.

> The Prince advised her (on her saying, like a good child, 'What *am* I to do another time?') to behave like an opera-dancer after a pirouette, and always show all her teeth in a fixed smile. Of course, he accompanied the advice with an immense pirouette and prodigious grin of his own, such as few people could perform just after dinner without being sick, ending on one foot, and t'other in the air.

So much for the legend of Albert as the heavy, humourless German: he and Victoria were well-matched.

CHAPTER IV

High Life at Court

Queen Victoria's Court has been much criticised for its stiffness and emphasis on etiquette—a typical story is of the Queen saying to a nursing mother, 'I know you are not very strong yet, Lady —; so I beg you will sit down, and when the Prince comes in, Lady — will stand in front of you'. In fact, by comparison with foreign Courts of the day, Victoria's was simple and easy-going. 'If Queen Victoria's Drawing Rooms sound elaborate, they were simplicity itself compared with the pomp and circumstance of corresponding occasions in Berlin,' declared Princess Marie Louise. Vienna was even worse. The Queen herself took pride in the fact that her Court was considered 'a pattern of *right dignity without stiffness*'. Provided she retained the 'right dignity' she was prepared to bend the rules. From the beginning her kindness kept breaking through. When her 'Uncle Sussex' came with an official deputation 'he offered to bend the knee and kiss her hand (which is the regular form on such occasions) but she immediately stopped him, put her arms round his neck and kissed his cheek'. Almost the first act of her reign was to address a letter of condolence to 'Queen Adelaide'. When it was pointed out that this should be 'The Queen Dowager' her reply was: 'I know that, but I shall not be the first to remind her of it.' When Adelaide, herself a stickler for such things, came to dinner she was 'quite shocked at the idea of going in before me, but I insisted on it'. (Queen Victoria was again to be insistent with the widowed ex-Empress Eugénie. Going in to dinner they would perform a little comedy of manners: '*Après vous, ma soeur*'—'*Non, après vous, ma soeur.*')

After Albert's arrival on the scene breaches of etiquette con-
tinued to occur. For instance, when P. T. Barnum took Tom
Thumb to the Palace Court officials told him he must address the
Queen through a lord-in-waiting. This he found difficult to do.

> Two or three questions were put and answered through the
> process indicated in my drill. It was a round-about way of doing
> business, and I suppose the Lord-in-Waiting was seriously
> shocked, if not outraged, when I entered directly into con-
> versation with Her Majesty. She, however, seemed not disposed
> to check my boldness, for she immediately spoke directly to me
> in obtaining the information she sought. I felt entirely at ease in
> her presence...

Similar thoughts occurred to Van Amburgh's clown. After a
most affable reception by Queen and Prince he was moved to
suggest that their manner 'might be copied by some of our grocers
and muffin-makers to their great improvement'.

Both etiquette and moral standards at Court were inherited by
Queen Victoria. During King William's time, for instance, it had
been noted that, in the tradition of Queen Charlotte, Queen
Adelaide 'will not receive in her Drawing Room anyone with the
slightest taint on their reputations'. Early on Victoria consulted
Melbourne about someone Adelaide had excluded who now
wished to be received. 'It will not do,' he advised, 'for you to
reverse a sentence passed by the late Court in the beginning of
your reign.'

Furthermore at the time of the Queen's accession the moral
fervour that was to become a distinctive feature of the Victorian
age was already running strong. Melbourne, though he detested
'this damned morality', saw the way things were going:

> Talked of Uncle's thinking I ought to play at cards, which
> Lord M. thought quite a mistake; of George III's playing
> Commap and Backgammon on a Sunday, which Lord M.
> said would *now* be thought very wrong. George III was very
> religious, Lord M. said, but against anything puritanical. 'When
> Bishop Porteus came to remonstrate with him,' he continued,

'about his going to Windsor on a Sunday, he received him with his carriage at the door.'

Queen Victoria was like her grandfather in many ways, and was certainly no more puritanical than he was. She distinguished, for instance, between good and evil intentions. When Lord Palmerston ('Cupid' to his friends), having an assignation with a lady at Windsor Castle, entered the wrong lady's bedroom and attempted to seduce her, the Queen was justifiably shocked. But when Guizot, the French Ambassador, lost in the maze of Castle corridors, got by mistake into another lady's room, she was amused:

He spent nearly an hour about the corridors to try and identify his bedroom. At length he opened a door which he imagined led to it; but before he advanced many steps in the room he discovered that a lady was seated before the toilet table with a maid brushing her hair. The abashed gentleman made a hasty retreat, and was fortunate when he returned to the bewildering corridors to find a guide who took him to his own room. The incident had almost passed from his mind when the following evening he was reminded of it by a laughing allusion made by the Queen. M. Guizot then discovered that it was Her Majesty's dressing room he had entered.

Her sense of proportion and tolerant attitude were evident in a letter she wrote to Albert before their marriage. 'I like Lady A— very much,' she told him, 'only she is a little too *strict and particular*, too severe towards others, which is not right; for I think one ought always to be indulgent towards other people, *as I always think, if we had not been well brought up and taken care of, we might also have gone astray*.' 'It is always right,' she added, 'to show that one does not like to see what is obviously wrong; but it is very dangerous to be too severe.' These feelings, formulated when she was an unmarried girl, she was to retain all her life. They did not perhaps match the stricter standards of Victorian middle-class morality, but then Queen Victoria was never a typical Victorian. Nor, though her behaviour might be copied by the middle classes,

would she have regarded her outlook in any way 'middle-class'.
She had in fact fewer points of contact with middle class people
than she had with either the aristocracy or with servants.

Her own religious faith was of a simple, tolerant, liberal kind.
As Melbourne once said, she 'very much disliked being talked *at*
upon religion; she particularly disliked what Her Majesty termed
a *Sunday face*'. She and Albert watched the development of what
came to be known as the 'English Sunday' with undisguised
horror. Nevertheless, they felt obliged to make concessions to the
sabbatarian movement. Bishop Wilberforce noticed in 1845, for
instance, that on Saturday cards were played at Court, but on
Sunday there was only chess. (Wilberforce still regretted the
chess!) Later on the Queen felt it necessary to warn her newly-
married eldest daughter of the likely effect of her intention to
make a Sunday theatre visit her first engagement in Berlin: 'Many
over here hold the most extreme views on religious observance
of "The Day of the Lord" (views which I never could share).' 'You
know that I am not at all an admirer or approver of our very dull
Sundays,' she later added, 'for I think the absence of innocent
amusement for the poor people a misfortune and an encouragement to vice.'

From time to time she would fight rearguard actions in defence
of such innocent amusements. One late Victorian biographer was
shocked to find her boasting in the late 1850s that she had 'arranged
a little dance in a tent on Sunday (which was very successful)'.
When Sir Benjamin Hall, the Minister who gave his name to
Big Ben, arranged for military bands to play in Kew Gardens on
Sundays, she was amongst his most enthusiastic supporters.
Nevertheless, the idea had to be dropped because of formidable
opposition. When a campaign was started to stop Sunday postal
deliveries a forthright interpretation of divine intentions was
despatched to the Prime Minister: 'The Queen thinks it a very
false notion of obeying God's will to do what will be a cause of
much annoyance and possibly of great distress to private families.'
The House of Commons' objection to the Sunday opening of
museums had her up in arms again. She was on the side of the

underdog: 'It is very well for those people who have no hard work during the week to go two or three times to church on Sunday and remain quiet for the rest of the day, but as regards the working class the practice is perfect cruelty.'

Nor did she share the views of Mrs. Proudie on Sunday travel. She travelled herself on Sunday and expected others in her service to do so. One of her Prime Ministers, Lord Rosebery, discovered this to his cost when she arranged for one of his visits to Windsor to end on a Sunday. On his way home one of his carriage horses lost a shoe and he had to proceed at a foot's pace to the nearest forge in the face of 'the freezing looks of the church-goers along the road, who eyed me as if I were the Scarlet Lady of Babylon herself, instead of a guest returning from a visit to his Sovereign'.

In some respects Queen Victoria was more enlightened than her mother. Though the Duchess of Kent was addicted to shilling whist, she drew the line at her daughter's penchant for novels. As the Queen once told Lord Melbourne, 'Mamma admonished me for reading light books'. In this category the Duchess apparently included *Oliver Twist*. Albert was not free from criticism either. When one evening in later years he began singing comic songs at the drawing-room piano with Princess Alice and Eleanor Stanley, the Duchess, says Lady Eleanor, 'did not feel it quite proper to hear him with the two young ladies, and was only reconciled to it by the reflection that one of them was his daughter'.

Albert was not above having a little fun at his mother-in-law's expense, as the young Mr. Gladstone observed. Rabusse was being played and 'the Prince kept trying to put out the Duchess of Kent, in fun, and she as constantly appealed to him in German not to make her confused'. Another time Eleanor Stanley heard him drily poking fun:

Last night was played Blind Hookey, a horrid gambling game, for pence. And the Duchess of Kent quite innocently asked: 'Blind Hookey? What is dat game?' 'I don't know,' said the Prince, 'only he is Hookey, and he is blind.' So we laughed, it was said so *gravely*, and quite puzzled the Duchess.

The playing of card games, on which Melbourne had had reservations, became common practice at Court about the time the old man resigned as Prime Minister. Up to this point Albert had normally played chess of an evening. Now, noted his Private Secretary, 'instead of her usual conversation with her old Prime Minister some round game at cards is substituted'. 'The Prince', he added, 'to amuse the Queen at this has nearly left off his chess.' Albert would have preferred to have had more literary and scientific men at Court, but his wife frankly admitted she had 'no fancy for learned discourses'. Simple games and amusing conversation suited her much better. So Vingt-et-un and Commerce and Nain Jaune held sway.

To make matters worse in the eyes of Victorian moralists play was soon for money albeit small stakes.

> We had a delightful evening yesterday [reported Eleanor Stanley] being summoned to the royal table, and playing Commerce. It was not quite as it is usually played; there is no pool, and nobody died, but the lowest hand of each deal put in a shilling . . . The fun was to see Lady Charlemont playing, as she did not at all understand the game . . . she kept us in subdued fits the whole time, and nobody dared advise her, as the Prince said any person guilty of such an offence should pay sixpence . . .
>
> . . . yesterday they had a merry round game, and went into fits at each other's mistakes, the Queen and Lord Morpeth's laugh being most conspicuous . . .

Even the up-and-coming Mr. Gladstone, upright and religious though he was, got drawn into this gambling net. 'After dinner,' he told his wife, 'we went to cards and played Commerce—fortunately I was never the worse hand, and so was not called upon to pay for I had locked up my purse before going to dinner—and I found I had won 2/2 at the end, 8d of which was payed me by the Prince.' At a later session, though, he was not so lucky—'I lost 8d at a game called rabusse'—not bad training, perhaps, for a future Chancellor of the Exchequer.

More than one observer was forcibly struck by the Queen's unfailing ability to be amused by simple things. 'We had riddles and charades, of which I proposed one or two that I recollected from the old days,' Lord Broughton later recalled, 'H.M. was much pleased and entered into the spirit of these trifling games much quicker, as I thought, than the other ladies.' Eleanor Stanley confirms this view:

> I went with the Queen and the Prince last night to the Haymarket Theatre to see the *Beef and Orange*, a fairy tale plot, and awfully stupid, as Lady Canning and I agreed, but the Royal couple laughed very much and seemed to enjoy it of all things. It is certainly a nice thing about them that they are so easily amused.

Theatre visits were a favourite form of recreation. French plays were particular favourites. Later the Queen's eldest daughter asked about the propriety of young married women seeing such things. Queen Victoria replied without hesitation:

> . . . as regards the French plays—you should go; there are many —indeed quantities of charming little plays—and dear Papa— who you know is anything but favourable to the French—used to delight in going to the French play—more than to any other, and we used for many years—when we had a good company here (we have had none since '54) to go continually and enjoyed it excessively.

During the early years of the reign the English theatre was at a low ebb. 'The Opera was respectable,' recorded one theatrical historian, 'and Shakespeare, when performed by Macready or Charles Kean, might become so, but melodrama was not polite, and Queen Victoria was severely criticised for attending *The Corsican Brothers* at the Princess's.' Such criticism, though, did not stop further royal visits to melodrama, and to light comedy and farces. Actually Queen Victoria preferred such entertainment to heavier stuff.

Nevertheless she and Albert took it upon themselves, as Victoria told the King of Prussia in 1849, 'to revive and elevate English drama which has greatly deteriorated through lack of support by Society'. 'We are having,' she explained, 'a number of performances of classical plays in a small, specially constructed theatre in the castle.' Thereafter, till the Prince died, such performances, with a particular emphasis on Shakespeare, were a regular occurrence. In fact Queen Victoria in these years took a keener and more active interest in the theatre than any British monarch since Charles II. The effect of continuous royal patronage during the Prince's lifetime was to help bring the theatre out of the doldrums. Accordingly when in later years the Queen renewed her interest she found the London theatre both flourishing and respectable.

Victoria's theatrical interest did not limit itself to artistic merit. Throughout her life she was fascinated by the appearance and general demeanour of those she saw on the stage. The French actress Rachel, when she came to London, was accorded both royal patronage and royal scrutiny. 'We are so pleased with Mme. Rachel,' the Queen then reported—'She is perfect, *et puis*, such a nice modest girl.' Rachel's love life proved to be neither nice nor modest, but this made no difference to royal patronage. The same interest was displayed in Jenny Lind who, much to Grisi's disgust, became the new singing sensation in London.

> To-night [wrote the Queen] we are going to the Opera in state, and will hear and see Jenny Lind (who is perfection) in *Norma*, which is considered one of her best parts. Poor Grisi is quite going off, and after the pure angelic voice and extremely quiet, perfect acting of J. Lind, she seems quite passée. Poor thing! she is quite furious and was excessively impertinent to J. Lind.

Among the men Mario continued to be a great favourite. He was 'so handsome' the Queen was to recall, and his voice 'most heavenly'. He was best, she thought, in *Les Huguenottes*, singing *Tu m'ami*. 'We used to go again and again to the Opera, only for that scene.'

Even though some of them might feel she was too easily amused, the Queen's attendants were devoted to her. Sometimes it was her thoughtfulness they found touching. 'So dull for you, Mary, to come upstairs,' she said to a young Maid of Honour as they were leaving a ball, 'Do go back, my dear, and dance as much as you like.' At other times it was the intense personal interest she displayed in their families. Visiting statesmen, too, were struck by her affability. Lord Warwick, indeed, was so intrigued by her jokes that he cried when resigning from Peel's government. Lord Macaulay, with his own propensity for jokes, found himself in great demand. 'When we came out of the drawing room the Queen came up to me with great animation, and insisted on my telling her some of my stories, which she had heard second hand . . .' He did not disappoint her—'I certainly made her laugh heartily'. He had in fact been a source of royal mirth since Melbourne's day when Sydney Smith had called him 'a book in breeches'. Once the Queen offered him a horse to ride, but, as he was such an unsteady rider, this merely produced the retort 'If I ride anything it must be an elephant.'

Sometimes, though, contact with statesmen was amusing only in retrospect. The Duke of Wellington, for example, had all his faculties but was becoming so deaf, Lady Lyttelton found, as to be positively embarrassing:

> Last evening was amusing enough thanks to the Duke of Wellington who made a great joke by beginning to talk as loud as thunder to the Queen, by whom he sat, about a matter of such serious and critical and difficult state importance, that it ought only to have been alluded to in *Cabinet*. He was evidently quite unaware of how loud he talked. The Queen blushed over and over, and at last succeeded in screaming out upon some other subject. But he went on: 'Yes Madam. That is what I am driving at now. Whether I shall carry my point I am not sure.'

To Lady Lyttelton the prospect of a visit from the Queen's old uncle, the Duke of Cambridge, was equally unnerving:

> I am going to dine down to help work off the old Duke of Cambridge, who is said to be somewhat troublesome, by asking

in his good Father's tone such questions as, 'How do you get on here? Rather dull, hey?' within two chairs of the Queen at a small table . . . The Duke of Cambridge at Chatsworth the other day, on his knees, in the middle of family prayers, very loud before the assembled household, 'A d—d good custom this!'

After such troublesome guests it was a relief for the Queen to welcome interesting artists. John Gibson, the sculptor, was much impressed.

Gibson had been telling the Queen how some lady dressed her hair with a roll-over, down low on her neck . . . and she immediately exclaimed, 'Would you like to see my hair dressed so?' and finding he would she jumped down from the high chair and ran out of the room singing, followed by her Lady. In a quarter of an hour she returned. 'Now,' she said 'is this right?'

Her reaction to his request to measure her mouth confirms her high spirits.

'Oh, certainly you may,' laughingly replied Her Majesty; 'that is, if I can only keep still and not laugh.' The request was so novel that it was a long time before he was successful.

Landseer and Winterhalter were favourites with both Queen and Prince. Landseer gave them tips on painting and taught them to etch, hobbies from which they derived keen enjoyment. Thorburn, as Victoria laughingly informed her ladies, was at first less successful in interpreting the royal taste.

She made us all laugh by telling us that when she sat for Thorburn for the first time, she and the Prince had a great deal of trouble about the attitude in which Princess Alice, who was sitting in the Queen's lap, should be painted in, as they did not like Thorburn's idea which was to have her arms spread out; so that the child was really in the shape of a cross; and when the picture was finished, and they observed this to him, he said,

'Yes, I meant it to be allegorical, to represent the Church leaning on the bosom of the State (!!) . . .'

The Queen's bosom was the subject of much saucy comment. One wonders, for instance, what she thought on reading the report in *The Times* (not yet respectable) on one of her portraits. 'The Queen's bosom', it noted, 'has been most deliciously handled and has been brought out by the artist in full rotundity.'

CHAPTER V

Happy Families

Queen Victoria was appalled when, soon after her marriage, her Uncle Leopold tactlessly expressed the hope that she would eventually become '*Mamma d'une nombreuse famille*'. It is doubtful whether she enjoyed the process of conception. She certainly hated being pregnant. She *loathed* the process of childbirth. Nevertheless, between her twenty-first and thirty-eighth birthdays she succeeded in bringing nine children into the world. In 1840, after ten months of marriage, she gave birth to Victoria, the Princess Royal (later Crown Princess of Prussia and Empress Frederick of Germany), known in the family as 'Vicky'. In 1841, less than a year later, came 'Bertie', the Prince of Wales (later King Edward VII). Alice (later Grand Duchess of Hesse) arrived in 1843, and in 1844 there was Alfred, known as 'Affie', (later Duke of Edinburgh). Helena, known as 'Lenchen', (later Princess Christian of Schleswig-Holstein) was born in 1846, and Louise (later Duchess of Argyll) in 1848. Arthur (later Duke of Connaught) followed in 1850, and Leopold (later Duke of Albany) in 1853. Last of all, in 1857, came Beatrice (later Princess Henry of Battenberg), long known as 'Baby'.

Even after a child was born Queen Victoria was honest enough to admit some reservations. 'Abstractedly I have no *tendre* for them till they become a little human; an ugly baby is a very nasty object—and the prettiest is frightful—till about four months; in short as long as they have their big body and little limbs and that terrible froglike action.' Yet she loved her children dearly and was an uncommonly attentive mother. Considering her liking for other people's children it would have been odd if she had not cared for her own. If anything she and Albert were over-conscientious and over-anxious. When, for instance, the Prince of Wales' lethargic habits did not augur well for the future they were beside themselves with worry and seized on Baron Stockmar's advice to try and educate him into a good life. They were not alone in those days in believing that education and a regulated life could work miracles. (George III had had the same illusions.) In fact the strict régime simply confirmed the young prince's taste for pleasure and self-indulgence. Yet he never went completely off the rails—as his own over-indulged eldest son, Albert Victor, was to threaten to do—and he always regarded his father and mother with affection. For he could never question their motives nor forget the happy times he had had as a child.

Victoria and Albert had themselves both been the victims of unnatural childhoods, she without a father and he without a mother. They were therefore determined that their children should grow up happily, surrounded by security and affection. Their attitude was scarcely typical of royal and aristocratic families of the period. Children of such families were, not only not heard, but generally rarely seen. The Queen and Prince acted on the twin principles of having their children with them whenever possible, and of being on a confidential basis with them. An early criticism was that they snatched them away from their lessons too often. The Queen made it a practice to play with them every afternoon and visited them in their rooms before she dressed for dinner. The consequence of such interest was that when Prince Frederick William of Prussia came on a visit he was amazed at the easy and happy relationship that existed between parents and children.

Although the hoped-for heir was not the first to arrive, no child has been made more welcome than the little Princess Royal. 'I think you would be amused to see Albert dancing her in his arms,' Uncle Leopold was told, 'he makes a capital nurse'. And later, 'Victoria plays with my old bricks, & C., and I see her running and jumping in the flower beds, as *old*, though I fear still *little* Victoria of former days used to do.'

Partly as a result of so much attention the child soon became extremely precocious. At a year her mother reported her as 'coquetting with the Hussars at either side of the carriage', and as time went on her 'old-fashioned' ways added extra enjoyment to Court life. As Eleanor Stanley told her mother,

> I have really enjoyed this waiting, seeing so much of the Royal couple, and the little Princess Royal is always there, and yesterday she made a great acquaintance with me, and was very curious to know why I had *only*!!! three flounces on my lilac gown. I said I thought it was quite enough, in which opinion the Queen, who was standing by much amused, quite agreed.

Later, when the Queen read to her daughter that 'God created man in his own image', the effect was not what was intended. Recalling a very ugly royal secretary, the child piped up, 'But, Mamma, surely not Dr. Prätorious?'

The Prince of Wales turned out to be less bright than his sister but he too provided moments of mirth. 'Pray, Mamma,' he asked his mother, 'is not a pink the female of a carnation?' 'Poor darling!' remarked Lady Lyttelton, 'I am sorry he said it, for he got such shouts of laughter.' No more, though, than Lady Lyttelton herself, promoted to the post of Governess, after Archdeacon Wilberforce asked whether he might see the young prince:

> Said I to the Queen yesterday morning, 'Madam! Mr. Wilberforce has asked leave to see the Prince of Wales—may he?' 'Oh yes, by all means,' and then after a little pause, 'I think he looked rather ill last night.' Upon which the governess had the wit to reply 'Why, Ma'am, he certainly was rather fretful at bedtime.' And Her Majesty had meant the Archdeacon . . . Think of the joke against poor me!

Winter brought special pleasures with the children in which the Governess was able to join:

> This morning we had a very pretty and brilliant amusement. The Queen took the Princess Royal, with me to hold her, in the sledge, the Prince driving. The sledge is quite pretty; beautiful

grey ponies all covered with bells and sparkling harness; the
gentlemen attending, and scarlet grooms preceding and following, over the dazzling snow, in the purest sunshine.

Intensely sentimental, Albert loved Christmas. It was he who
popularised in Britain the old German custom of the Christmas
tree. Christmas was always spent at Windsor where the rooms
were filled with enormous fir trees decorated with candles and
sweetmeats.

Nor was Albert above turning somersaults with his children,
or dragging them round the room in a basket, or swinging the
youngest in his table napkin. He would fly kites with them,
'noisily and eagerly'. Coming across his sons playing football
when he was out walking with the Queen, he stopped and joined
in the game. Even later, when the Prince of Wales was eighteen
and Albert a prematurely-aged forty, he did not miss the fun when
it came to building a snowman and making a slide for the sledge.

Victoria shared this desire to amuse the children. She loved to
teach them games. One account shows how innocently Georgiana
Liddell won favour at Court—'by teaching her Royal Mistress to
make a mouse out of a pocket-handkerchief, and to cause it to run
about her arm and hand'. Another pleasure the Queen was keen
her children should share was her own love of dancing. She helped
teach them the steps and gave special dances for them. In 1854, for
instance, she gave a children's ball at Buckingham Palace. 'Magnificent' was an adult's description of it; 'capital fun', thought one
of the young participants. The Prime Minister of the day received
what must be one of the most unusual letters a Head of Government has ever received from his Sovereign. 'Though the Queen
cannot send Lord Aberdeen *a card for a children's ball*,' wrote
Victoria, 'perhaps he may not disdain coming for a short while to
see a number of happy little people, including some of his grandchildren, enjoying themselves.' Eleanor Stanley observed how the
Queen helped these affairs go with a swing, 'fussing about getting
partners for her little girls and arranging them in quadrilles just
like any of the other Mamas, and then taking a turn in the waltz

with the Prince of Wales, and then one with the Princess Royal'. She did not stand on ceremony. When she saw Gladstone's young daughter and Sidney Herbert's son having difficulty in leading a country dance she rushed down 'and held our hands across and showed us how to pirouette'. But it was the young Duke of Argyll who hit upon the royal formula for making these occasions a success: the Queen enjoyed them as much as the children.

The Queen and Prince Albert danced a great deal. We had a dance called 'the grandfather', and when it was their turn they took the ends of a handkerchief, and went down the row, and we all jumped over the handkerchief. The Queen laughed much as we jumped.

Any excuse was good enough for a party. On Prince Alfred's thirteenth birthday 'a band played, and after dinner we danced, with the three boys and three girls, a merry country dance on the terrace'. The New Year had to be welcomed in, and when nine-year-old Prince Arthur looked 'so miserable' at bedtime his mother sent a message asking his governor 'whether he had better not remain until a ¼ to 11'. A full-scale party was even thrown for Princess Beatrice's second birthday, and 'very successful' it was according to her mother. 'They could of course not speak to each other but were very droll.'

On special occasions the children were encouraged to put on *tableaux vivants* and theatrical performances. Eleanor Stanley was present at the Queen's fourteenth wedding anniversary celebrations, and was struck by the natural child-parent relationship.

We saw the royal children act their *tableaux* yesterday afternoon, which we had much wished to do; it was all Lady Caroline's doing, as the Queen, not knowing exactly what was coming, and how it would go off, was nervous and had not meant to let a soul come and see it . . .

Lady Caroline told them she had seen the rehearsal and it was so pretty, and the children looked so well that she really thought she might take upon herself to say that they would have no cause to regret letting anyone be present; upon which they said very well; but the Prince said if they asked one visitor they must ask all, which was agreed to . . . so they were sent for and it began directly.

The scenes were the four seasons, Princess Alice as Spring, scattering flowers, and speaking an appropriate little speech out of Thomson's *Seasons*; the curtain fell, and presently rose again showing Prince Arthur in a very short and scanty blue frock asleep on the ground, and the Princess Royal as Summer, in a rosy light, oppressed as it were with heat; she spoke a little speech too out of the *Seasons*; and then, after a short interval, we had a third scene Autumn, Prince Alfred as Bacchus, in a Leopard skin and crowned with grapes; and then Winter, Prince of Wales as an old man warmly dressed and icicles hanging about his coat and hat . . .

Afterwards Prince Arthur's short frock, says Lady Eleanor, scandalised his mother. 'The Queen was so shocked at Prince Arthur's scanty attire (though his nurse assured her he had 'flesh-coloured decencies' on) that she sent him away to be dressed, but when he came back all the difference I saw was a pair of socks that hardly came above his ankles.' As Arthur was only four years old at the time this bears witness to his mother's excessive sense of modesty, something she possessed all her life. An even more shocking incident involving children caused her acute embarrassment during a stay at the home of Lord Abercorn when one of his boys, wearing a kilt, insisted on standing on his head as if to prove to her that he had nothing on underneath.

Yet, curiously, the Queen did not carry her feelings of modesty into the world of art. When a collection of nude statues was installed in the Crystal Palace at Sydenham prior to its opening by Victoria, it was not she or Albert who objected. It was the bishops, and they threatened to boycott the ceremony unless something was done. Someone saucily suggested to Albert that the bishops might care to lend their aprons to effect a cover-up job. Eventually a sufficiency of fig-leaves was provided to quieten episcopal consciences. The Queen and Prince, on the other hand, were in the

habit of exchanging nude pictures, something which Compton
Mackenzie was to discover many years later when he went to
Buckingham Palace to be knighted.

On the walls of the last corridor was a large picture of an almost
nude Artemis; I had just asked myself what Queen Victoria
would have said to such a picture hanging in Buckingham
Palace when I read the inscription underneath: 'it was one of the
young Queen Victoria's wedding presents to Prince Albert.'

CHAPTER VI

The Changing Scene

Young Queen Victoria loved a change of scene and after her marriage continued her former practice of making occasional visits to the great houses of the aristocracy. Though these trips were carefully organised by her hosts, the unexpected incident could usually be relied on to add to her pleasure. During a ball in her honour at Wimpole, for example, an officer on escort duty witnessed two episodes that amused her.

> My cousin, Lord Caledon, then in the Guards, was told early in the evening that he was destined to have the honour of dancing with Her Majesty, which threw him into an agony of apprehension. He entreated me to retire with him into one of the embrasures of the dancing hall and give him some idea of the steps. Accordingly, providing ourselves with a bottle of champagne, we retired from observation and commenced my lesson . . .
>
> The *tableau* had evidently been communicated to the Queen, for she laughed heartily when he came up, looking like a malefactor led out for instant execution, and proceeded with scrupulous fidelity, as best he could, to perform the steps he had just learned.

The other incident involved a couple who were this time too keen on dancing and invaded part of the floor reserved for Victoria:

> Not observing the Queen, he said 'Holloa! there is no one here;' and dashed in waltzing in a somewhat eccentric manner, with his elbows stuck out. He just escaped coming against Her

Majesty, who was seated. We rushed forward to stop them dancing, when the Queen said 'Let them stay—they are very amusing.' When they finished dancing they found themselves directly opposite Her Majesty whose eyes were fixed firmly on them. Their consternation was very great, and they fled precipitately amid general laughter.

When Victoria and Albert went to Stafford (now Lancaster) House it was, as a future Duke of Argyll recorded, the children who provided the amusement:

We were to precede the party as they walked up the stairs of the great central hall, and were to do it backwards. But only one rehearsal had been undertaken. All went pretty well until half the ascent had been accomplished, and then one, afraid of tripping up, ignominiously turned tail, followed by the other three, to the great amusement of the Queen, who laughed much at us.

The future Earl of Warwick remembered an even worse mishap providing light relief during his boyhood at Warwick Castle:

. . . While going over the Castle with the Queen my mother brought her to her new boudoir then in the course of being finished. My mother's kinswoman, old Lady Mexborough, was with us, and the Queen, who knew she was even older than she looked, said to her very kindly: 'Please sit down.'

Lady Mexborough thereupon sat down in one of the new and incomplete chairs that had not been seated and her partial disappearance was very swift and dramatic. Queen Victoria's strict sense of decorum was not quite proof against the incident.

Although the Queen did not care for anything as cold and deliberate as a practical joke she certainly had a taste for unrehearsed slapstick, crude as this may sometimes appear. This taste was again in evidence during an incident at the Prince's Theatre. The manager was following tradition by walking backwards and carrying candles whilst showing her to her carriage. When he fell head over heels and covered himself in candle-grease Victoria leaned against the wall and broke into loud laughter.

Royal visits to Ireland brought different rewards. The Queen loved the exuberance of the Irish which remained apparently unaffected by the Great Famine only a few years before. She kept her eyes open for local colour and eccentricities. 'We drove out yesterday afternoon,' she told her Uncle Leopold during her 1849 visit, 'and were followed by jaunting-cars and riders and people running and screaming, which would have amused you.' Another day,

> ... after luncheon we walked out and saw some of the country dance jigs, which was very amusing. It is quite different from the Scotch reel; not so animated, and the steps different, but very droll. The people were very poorly dressed in thick coats, the women in shawls. There was one man who was a regular specimen of an Irishman, with his hat on one ear.

The women the Queen thought lovely, 'really very handsome ... such beautiful black eyes and hair and such fine colours and teeth'. They appear to have been equally impressed by the Queen's open and friendly manner. 'Oh, Queen, dear,' shouted one woman as the royal couple were out driving with their children, 'make one of them darlints Prince Patrick and all Ireland will die for you.' The cry did not go unheeded and Patrick was among the names she gave her next baby.

One of the few places Queen Victoria disliked was Brighton. She did not care for George IV's Pavilion—'a strange Chinese looking thing, haunted by ghosts best forgotten'. As a seaside retreat it was useless: 'I only see a little morsel of sea from one of my sitting room windows.' When she walked on the seafront, 'we were mobbed by all the shopboys in the town, who ran and looked under my bonnet, treating us just as they do the Band, when it goes on parade'. The same thing had happened when she tried to carry on the custom of walking in public on the North Terrace of Windsor Castle. Lady Lyttelton saw her surrounded by crowds 'as smiling and spirited as if *they* would do her no harm, till at last they fall back to make way for her'. Such mobbing was unpleasant and potentially dangerous. From these experiences evolved the practice of British royalty to take its exercise in private.

As the crowds became more persistent and the Royal Family increased in size Victoria and Albert became preoccupied with the need to find a country retreat. In 1845 they settled on Osborne in the Isle of Wight. It was, Victoria decided, 'a perfect little paradise', 'so snug and nice'. It was even better when a new mansion was built to Albert's designs. As the Queen wrote later, in her oddest English, Albert's plans 'were most admirably carried out by the late Mr. Thos Cubitt, than whom no better, kinder man did not exist'. Life there proved idyllic. Now Victoria discovered just how much she could enjoy what she called 'the solid pleasures of a peaceful, quiet, yet merry life in the country'. She discovered, too, a liking for simple country people. The unpretentiousness of their lives, and their frank, open manner struck a sympathetic chord in her nature that sophisticated society never did. All in all, rural pursuits, she decided, were 'far more durable than the amusements of London, though we don't despise or dislike these sometimes'.

Diplomatically the most important royal travels abroad in these years were the visits paid to the French monarchs Louis Philippe and Napoleon III. As was so often the case, the Queen felt 'very gay and amused', managing to combine affairs of State with private pleasure. On the way over to visit Louis Philippe for the first time Georgiana Liddell had an insight into this happy relaxed frame of mind, when Victoria was asked to move from her seat on deck.

'Move my seat,' said the Queen, 'why should I? What possible harm can I be doing here?'

'The fact is, Your Majesty is unwittingly closing the door of the place where the grog tubs are kept, and so the men cannot have their grog!'

'Oh, very well,' said the Queen, 'I will move on one condition, viz., that you bring me a glass of grog.'

This was accordingly done, and after tasting it the Queen said, 'I am afraid I can only make the same remark I did once before, that I think it would be very good if it were stronger!'

There was a similarly light-hearted reaction after her arrival when she was the subject of mistaken identity:

Victoria, visiting one of the French ships, liked some cakes extremely, and a parcel of them were sent over to the Royal yacht. When the messenger saw a woman on the yacht's deck dressed in a common-looking black gown, dark bonnet, and a plain red woollen shawl, he held out the packet saying, 'Take this, miss, they are cakes for the Queen. Take care of them! Now mind, don't fail to give them her'. It was the Queen herself, and she laughed heartily over the mistake.

In fact Queen Victoria loved being incognito, and absolutely revelled in being mistaken for someone else. Because of her un-pretentious mode of dress such mistakes were not uncommon. Old Lord Portarlington once greeted her with the words 'I know your face quite well, but dammit I cannot put a name to it'. 'One moonlit night,' says John Gore, 'she was leaning from her window at Windsor Castle, and was softly addressed by a sentimental sentry below. It was with the most full-blooded laughter that she related how "he mistook me for a housemaid". ' During her first stay at Holyroodhouse she was quite happy wandering about like an ordinary visitor—and was promptly mistaken for one.

We saw the rooms where Queen Mary lived, her bed, the dressing-room into which the murderers entered to kill Rizzio, and the spot where he fell, where, the old housekeeper said to me, 'if the lady would stand on that side', I would see that the boards were discoloured by the blood . . . The old housekeeper did not know who I was, and only learned it from Mr. Charles Murray afterwards.

During her visit to Napoleon III in 1855, the first by an English monarch to Paris for nearly 400 years, the Queen's unfashionable dress was much remarked on. The Emperor's cousin was appalled to see the Queen of England proudly carrying an enormous hand-bag on which one of her daughters had embroidered a gaudy parrot. At dinner General Canrobert, though much taken with her 'sweet expression' and natural behaviour, was appalled by the fussiness of her appearance.

> She wore geranium flowers placed here there and everywhere. She had plump hands with rings on every finger, and even on her thumbs; one of these contained a ruby of prodigious size and of a superb blood-red. She found it difficult to use her knife and fork with her hands thus laden with these reliquaries, and even more difficult to take off and put on her gloves.

This curious habit of loading herself with rings dated from before her marriage. Lord Melbourne had got quite cross about it. 'It is those consumed rings,' he said when she couldn't get her gloves off, 'I never could bear them.' The Queen excused herself on the grounds that she was 'fond of them, and that it improved an ugly hand'. 'Makes them worse,' Melbourne replied. Marriage obviously led to no improvement in this direction though she did come to rely increasingly on Albert's choice in clothes. 'I hate being troubled about dress,' she confessed when only twenty-three. Albert's fashion sense could hardly be described as chic and the Queen's ensembles in Paris were the consequence.

What did impress the Parisians was an indefinable regal quality combined with energy and good humour. 'Everyone raves at her grace and dignity,' Lord Clarendon confirmed, 'The constant smile takes the fancy of the people.' The visit took place in that very hot weather which already accompanied her public appearances so often that, as Palmerston told her in one of his ingratiating moods, it was 'proverbially called the Queen's weather'. She however, did not care for heat and Clarendon wondered at her ability to cope:

> Conceive her walking in the heat here an hour in the morning, going over the Tuileries, and then for 3½ hours perambulating

at the Hotel-de-Ville . . . She knocked up everybody; the Emperor went in a great distress for the last league. One of his suite, a very fat man, was so knocked up that he gasped— *'Je donnerais tout—tout—la Vénus de Milo y incluse, pour un verre de limonade!'*

Her spirited dancing, so different from the languid manner of Parisian society, also excited comment, but then dancing was always more than a polite exercise to Queen Victoria.

As always it was the simple and the unexpected which pleased her most. She enjoyed her 'incognito' visit to the Paris shops, *God Save the Queen* played as a polka at the Hotel-de-Ville, and the dogs at the hunting lodge of La Muette. 'Her Majesty honoured the dogs by patting their heads,' wrote a tongue-in-cheek reporter, 'They seemed deeply grateful for the distinguished attention and licked the Queen's feet in the most courtier like style.' Victoria herself took the trouble of recording the kind of incident which particularly caught her fancy.

Some *jeune filles,* dressed all in white with green wreaths, then asked permission to present me with a nosegay and some fruit, and they came accompanied by a *Curé.* One of them, a very young girl, began a long speech, bringing in our visit, the alliance, the Exposition etc., and stopped suddenly saying: *'Ah, mon Dieu!'* The Emperor and I proposed to relieve her by taking the nosegay from her and thanking her: but she would *not* give it up, and said: *'Attendez, je vais me rappeler,'* which nearly set us off; but she persevered and did recollect it.

She broke down, however, a second time; and then the *curé* who had evidently composed the speech burst forth with the finale of *'Vive la Reine d'Angleterre!'* which set the girl right again, and she continued *'Vive la Reine d'Angleterre, vive sa Demoiselle, vive son Prince Albert, vive l'Empereur, vive l'Impératrice, vive tout le monde!'*

We laughed much afterwards, for the effect was so funny, and yet the poor girl was much to be pitied, and admired for her courage and perseverance. She looked so frightened.

Altogether the Queen was in raptures over this visit. 'I am *delighted, enchanted, amused,* and *interested,* and think I never saw anything more *beautiful* or gay than Paris.' How much more interesting a venue it was than her only previous meeting with Louis Napoleon—at a public breakfast for wash-houses in the Fulham Road! Now he turned on all his charm for her benefit. Louis Philippe had been amusing enough: his 'liveliness and vivacity, and little impatiences' had been 'my delight and amusement'. But Napoleon III was fascinating, 'very extraordinary . . . I might almost say mysterious . . . almost romantic'—a combination she could never resist. Eugénie's grace and sweetness also made a great impression. The Queen was able to admire the Empress's beauty without a trace of jealousy. When the imperial couple paid a visit to England Victoria made her admiration very clear to the Prussian Royal Family who were apt to look down their royal noses at the imperial upstarts:

> The Empress really is most charming, not only because of her beauty (and I have never seen her more *en beauté*) but equally because of her graciousness, her intellect, her naïveté and kindness of heart; she is so pleasant and intelligent to talk to. Albert has a great respect for her, and the children adore her, particularly Vicky and Alfred. She and the Emperor have taken great notice of them and are very fond of young people altogether. At the ball the Emperor danced with Lenchen, who beaming with joy, clasped the Emperor very tightly *for fear of losing him,* or so Vicky affirms!

Later when Victoria and Albert paid a semi-private visit to Cherbourg gay little incidents were again lovingly chronicled by the Queen: how at the Chateau 'the somewhat tipsy mayor conducted us over it', and when their carriage stopped it was 'most amusing to see people running out with candles, which they held up trying to get a sight of us'. Again, the royal style of dress gave no clues: the local inhabitants had to gather round and ask '*Qui est donc la Reine?*' Such informality was exactly to the Queen's taste. She had little liking for the stiffness which, with military overtones, passed for entertainment in places like Berlin. These years with Albert certainly whetted her appetite for foreign travel, but when in later life this appetite returned it was to the liveliness and informality of the Warm South that she was irresistibly drawn.

CHAPTER VII

Discovering Scotland

In all the world Queen Victoria never discovered anywhere to equal Scotland in her affections. Her first taste of it was during her trip to Edinburgh in 1842. A railway link from London did not yet exist, so she travelled by sea. A warm Scottish welcome awaited her. 'I have never,' one spectator was later to reminisce, 'forgotten the Queen, who with the Prince Consort beside her, looked small and young but so beamingly happy.' Although the royal couple did not venture far afield they saw enough of Scottish customs and scenery to whet their appetite. At Dalkeith the Queen for the first time 'tasted the oatmeal porridge, which I think very good, and also some of the "Finnan haddies" '. At Dupplin their host put on an unscheduled exhibition of slap-stick which could not fail to appeal:

> We left Dalkeith on Monday, and lunched at Dupplin, Lord Kinnoul's, a very pretty place with quite a new house, and which poor Lord Kinnoul displayed so well as to fall head over heels down a steep bank, and was proceeding down another, if Albert had not caught him; I did not see it, but Albert and I nearly died laughing at the *relation* of it.

The Queen's 'terpsichorean' feelings discovered a new and exciting outlet in Scottish dancing. She returned south determined to master the new steps, though, as Eleanor Stanley discovered, there were initial difficulties.

> After dinner, before the gentlemen came in, we had great fun teaching H.M. to dance reels; she could not at all manage the

figure 8; she never got back to her place in time, and 'one, two three, hop' was altogether above her comprehension, she being too dignified ever to hop on one foot; which however is absolutely necessary in a reel. We laughed very much, however, and amused ourselves excessively.

Practice quickly led to an improvement. 'We had great fun yesterday evening before the gentlemen came in, teaching the Queen the reel of Tulloch, to the music of your *favourites* the bag-pipes,' Lady Eleanor was soon telling her mother, '—the Queen danced and skipped gloriously.' Soon Queen Victoria was as accomplished at dancing reels as she was quadrilles.

Not surprisingly, a second Scottish trip was arranged before long. Then it was that Victoria and Albert really discovered the Highlands. They stayed at Blair Atholl, and the Queen could hardly find superlatives enough to express her feelings. 'Independently of the scenery,' she decided 'there is a quiet, a retirement, a wildness, a liberty, and a solitude that had such a charm for us.' Albert was 'in perfect ecstasies'. Part of the attraction for him was that he was reminded of his old home in Coburg. (His down-to-earth brother later pooh-poohed the idea: there was not the remotest similarity.) Close to nature Albert could relax. 'I must confess,' he told his brother, 'that the reporter was right when he said "the Prince looked pleased with everything and everybody, and with himself too".'

After their return home this new royal enthusiasm communicated itself to the Court. 'I never remember seeing Her Majesty in such high spirits,' Georgiana Liddell reported. 'She was out deerstalking one day for nine hours, not allowed to speak above a whisper, and had to hide among the rocks and heather for fear of disturbing the herd.' Lady Lyttelton was assured 'very pleasantly' that 'Scotch air, Scotch people, Scotch hills, Scotch rivers, Scotch woods, are all far preferable to those of any other nation in or out of this world; that deer-stalking is the most charming of amusements, etc., etc.' Gone were the days when, the royal doctor having been accused of always having someone to push forward, the Queen had commented caustically, 'And a Scotchman at that'. From now on 'Scotchmen', and especially Highlanders, were special beings in Queen Victoria's estimation—'such chivalrous, fine active people'.

She and Albert were not satisfied till they had their own High-land home. In the early 1850s they settled for Balmoral and arranged, as at Osborne, for the old castle to be replaced by one designed by the Prince. Rebuilding, however, was delayed by a strike among the workmen. 'Strikes,' Albert told Stockmar, 'are quite the fashion now.' In the interim they lived on happily in the old building in a state of acute overcrowding and discomfort. Lord Malmesbury, living there as Minister in Attendance, was less happy than his hosts.

> The rooms were so small that I was obliged to write my des-patches on my bed and to keep the window constantly open to admit the necessary quantity of air . . . and my private secretary lodged three miles off. We played at billiards every evening, the Queen and the Duchess being constantly obliged to get up from their chairs to be out of the way of the cues. Noth-ing could be more cheerful and evidently perfectly happy than the Queen and the Prince, or more kind to everyone around them.

Lord Clarendon heartily disliked what he called 'this scramble of rural royalty'. The extent of the scramble can be gauged from the fact that one of the ladies-in-waiting, having to sleep in a nearby cottage, had her breakfast sent over in a wheelbarrow. An atten-dant minister might find himself discussing affairs of state with the Queen sitting on the edge of his bed. Yet Victoria appeared hardly to notice any discomfort. Malmesbury espied her happily lying down in the heather whilst out deerstalking. 'H.M.,' it was noted, 'quite accepts the idea of sitting for hours perishing on a pony going at a foot's pace and coming home frozen.' Cold and rain did not trouble her. The sight of one of her freezing ladies actually bulging with clothes simply made her laugh.

Little upsets were accepted without demur, as when Albert

shot a stag and 'I sat down to sketch, and poor Vicky, unfortunately, seated herself on a wasp's nest and was much stung'; or
when Alfred, 'always bent on self-destruction', tumbled down-
stairs and acquired 'a terribly black, green and yellow face'; or,
when riding up a mountainside, 'my little pony, being so fat,
panted dreadfully'; or when Albert, putting on a kilt for the first
time, found it so involved he arrived late for dinner.

When the new castle was completed she was delighted, for it
was 'my dearest Albert's own creation, own work, own building,
own laying out'. Even so it was not to everybody's taste. Lord
Rosebery thought the drawing room at Osborne was the ugliest
he had ever seen till he saw the one at Balmoral. The most peculiar
feature, according to Lord Clarendon, was 'tartanitis'.

Here everything is Scotch—the curtains, the carpets, the furni-
ture, are all different plaids, and the thistles are in such abun-
dance that they would rejoice the heart of a donkey if they
happened to *look like* his favourite repast, which they don't.
I am told that it is *de rigueur* to clothe oneself in tweed directly.

Although it was August the temperature did not add to Clarendon's enjoyment:

It is very cold here, and I believe my feet were frost-bitten at
dinner, for there was not a fire at all there, and in the drawing-
room there were two little sticks which hissed at the man who
attempted to light them, and the Queen, thinking, I suppose,
that they meant to burn had a large screen placed between the
royal nose and the unlighted wood. She seemed, I thought,
particularly grateful for such small jokes as my freezing state
enabled me to crack.

As much time as possible was spent out of doors. There was
beautiful scenery to enthuse over, there were outdoor pursuits for
relaxation. 'No queen,' Victoria concluded, 'has ever enjoyed
what I am fortunate enough to enjoy.' In addition she found the
straight-speaking Highlanders a great attraction. Those who
attended on the Royal Family were 'so amusing', she was pleased

to find, 'and really pleasant and instructive to talk to'. One outdoor attendant, young John Brown, was more than usually forthright in his manner:

> When we were going down Craig-na-Ban—which is very steep, and rough, Jane Churchill fell and could not get up again, (having got her feet caught in her dress) and Johnny Brown (who is our factotum and really the perfection of a servant for he thinks of everything) picked her up like *un scène de tragédie* and when she thanked him, he said, 'Your Ladyship is not so heavy as Her Majesty!' which made us laugh much. I said 'Am I grown heavier do you think?' 'Well, I think you are', was the plain spoken reply. So I mean to be weighed as I always thought I was light.

Not many royal personages would have tolerated such observations by a servant, yet it was the very honesty of his remarks, so bluntly expressed, that earned for John Brown Queen Victoria's lifelong regard. Equally there appears to have been something in the Queen's demeanour—her friendliness and lack of affectation— to which not only John Brown but the Scots in general responded. A clue to this understanding can be found in the story of the Scottish servant who saw her on her first visit to Edinburgh.

> 'Well, what did you think of her, John?' his master asked on his return.
> 'Troth, sir, I was terrible feared afore she came forrit—my heart was amaist in my mouth; but when she did come forrit, od, I wasna feared at a'; I jist looked at her, an she lookit at me, and she bowed her heid to me, an' I bowed my heid to her. Od, she's a real fine leddie wi' fient a bit o' pride aboot her.'

This directness enabled Victoria quickly to establish friendly relations with her poorer Highland neighbours. 'She is running in and out of the house all day,' Charles Greville soon reported. She loved this freedom to roam about and cottage visiting became a firm feature of Balmoral life. The spontaneity and bluntness of the local people delighted her. 'Really,' Victoria decided, 'the affection of these people, who are so hearty and so happy to see you, taking an interest in everything, is very touching and gratifying.'

Naturally the local children came in for their share of attention. Seeing them in the natural surroundings of their own homes enhanced the pleasure of visiting. 'Her Majesty's gracious mother-liness impressed me much,' wrote Patricia Lindsay, the Balmoral factor's daughter. 'She took such kindly notice of some little grandsons of my father who were with us; one, a very pretty little boy, she warmly admired and kissed warmly, a caress of which he was proud to his dying day.' 'Baby Farquharson was very charming,' runs another account, 'insisting on sitting on the Queen's knee, and bringing up his brothers to present them!' Poor children, as well as rich, recognised Queen Victoria's kindli-ness was genuine and took to her at once. Occasionally, though, there was difficulty with the grown-ups, as when the Queen's liberal views on Sunday observance clashed with local sab-batarianism. 'Ye're violatin' the Sabbath,' one shocked old woman told the Queen when she arrived with a gift one Sunday. When told that Christ had performed good deeds on the Sabbath the woman accepted the present but fired a parting shot: 'Ah wiel, then I dinna think ony mair of him for it'.

While Victoria retained her broad views the simplicity of the presbyterian form of worship greatly appealed to her. She im-mediately felt at home in Crathie Church, and, as Patricia Lindsay reveals, friendly relations were soon established between Castle and Manse:

One member of the congregation in those times used to excite much interest and amusement among strangers. This was the minister's collie, who was a regular attender at church, follow-ing Mr. Anderson to the pulpit steps and quietly lying down at the top. He was always a most decorous, though possibly somewhat somnolent listener, but he was also an excellent timekeeper, for if a sermon was a few minutes longer than usual Towser got up and stretched himself, yawning audibly.

When the Queen first came Mr. Anderson feared she might

object to such an unorthodox addition to the congregation, and shut Towser up on Sunday. Her Majesty next day sent an equerry to the Manse to enquire if anything had happened to the dog, as she had a sketch of the interior of the church in which he appeared lying beside the pulpit, and if he were alive and well, she would like to see him in his old place. Greatly to Towser's delight he was thus by royal command restored to Church privileges.

There was further pleasure to be had, says Patricia Lindsay, from the peculiarities of visiting clergymen.

On one such occasion an elderly minister unknown to the Queen was to officiate, and she asked my father if he was acquainted with him. He replied in the affirmative, adding that he was an excellent man, highly esteemed in the Church, but that he had a peculiar pronunciation, as, for instance, in the words 'Clap your hands' he always said 'Clip your hens'.

By a strange chance the opening psalm selected on the Sunday was the forty-seventh, and my father often told how when the minister stood up and gave out 'All people clip your hens,' Her Majesty turned round with a humorous glance of appreciative recollection of his story.

Probably the greatest single source of enjoyment of these Highland holidays was the occasional extended excursion, what the Queen called 'great expeditions'. Though she was nearly 40 at the time Victoria recounted her adventures on one such trip with all the enthusiasm of a schoolgirl:

We decided to call ourselves Lord and Lady Churchill and party, Lady Churchill passing as Miss Spencer, and General Grey as Dr. Grey! Brown once forgot this, and called me "Your Majesty" as I was getting into the carriage; Grant on the box called Albert "Your Royal Highness," which set us off laughing but no one observed it.

. . . the people (at the inn) were very amusing about us. The woman came in while they were at their dinner, and said to

Grant, 'Dr. Grey wants you,' which nearly upset the gravity of all the others: then they told Jane, 'Your lady gives no trouble'.

Far from giving trouble the Queen was enraptured by everything, down to the breakfast of 'good tea and bread and butter, and some excellent porridge'. The accompanying discomforts she was happy to overlook. Others wondered at her ability to do so:

The Queen came back on Wednesday night in high glee with her lark over the hills to Grantown. They slept at a very little Highland inn, and were waited on by the maid only. The beds were awful, for they could not stand the feather bed, and, that being thrown aside, nothing soft remained underneath . . . However they were in high glee, and were not found out till they went away in the morning, when the man of the house said, 'Gin I'd known it was the Queen, I'd hae put on my Sunday claiths and waited on her mysel'.

On another excursion a crowd gathered round suspecting who they were, but 'Grant and Brown kept them off the carriages, and gave them evasive answers, directing them to the wrong carriages which was most amusing'. One trip shortly before the Prince's death was marred only by the spartan fare at the inn. 'Unfortunately,' Victoria lamented, 'there was hardly anything to eat, and there was only tea, and two miserable starved Highland chickens, without any potatoes!' There was, as she succinctly put it, 'no pudding and no *fun*'. The attendants fared even worse: 'They had only the remnants of our two starved chickens!'

If Edward VII's spiritual home was Paris his mother's was in the mountains of Scotland. 'Every year,' she admitted, 'my heart becomes more fixed in this dear Paradise.' Every year her inclination was to tarry longer and longer. Like so many things it brought out the little girl in her. As she confessed before one return journey south, 'I wished we might be snowed up and unable to move . . .'

CHAPTER VIII

The Last Years with Albert

A spectacular event marked the mid-way point of the Queen's married life. It was the Great Exhibition of 1851 which Albert played a vital part in promoting. Opposition was formidable. *The Times* expressed feelings of outrage that the exhibition building, the Crystal Palace, would turn Hyde Park into 'something between Wolverhampton and Greenwich Fair'. In the House of Commons local residents were advised 'to keep a sharp look out over their silver forks and spoons and servant maids', an odd order of priorities even for those days.

Small wonder that in the face of such obstacles when opening day arrived one of the most notable features at the initial ceremony was 'the radiant happiness of the Queen in seeing the success of her husband's great idea'. But, as with the best organised events, the unexpected happened. During the inevitable *Hallelujah Chorus* Victoria noticed that 'a Chinese mandarin came forward and made his obeisance'. But who was he? No-one seemed to know. The Lord Chamberlain, says Lord Playfair, not wishing to create an international incident over precedence, consulted the Queen and Prince.

We were then told there must be no mistake as to his rank, and that it would be best to place him between the Archbishop of Canterbury and the Duke of Wellington. In this dignified position he marched through the building to the delighted amazement of all beholders. Next day we ascertained that this Chinaman was the keeper of a Chinese junk that had been sent over to lie in the river Thames and which anyone could visit on the payment of a shilling!

Lord Playfair bears witness to the persistence of the Queen's enthusiasm which led her to visit the exhibition over forty times. He was present when one of the exhibitors put his foot in it. A highly nervous engraver was showing her a sample of his work which appears to have anticipated Picasso. It portrayed a boy jumping out of a boat watched by a large eye. Naturally curious, Victoria asked what it meant.

The reply was startling. 'The boy, madam, is the Prince of Wales and the eye is the Eye of God looking out with pleasure for the moment when His Royal Highness will land on his kingdom and become the reigning Sovereign!'
The gentlemen in attendance were aghast, but the Queen persevered her countenance till we left the stall, when both she and the Prince Consort laughed heartily. The latter told me that he only knew of one parallel incident. George IV had taken a fancy to a beautiful but silly young lady, and had her frequently near him. On asking her whether she was pleased with the Court festivities, she replied that she was, but that she was dying to see a coronation.

On another visit Victoria's inquisitiveness nearly caused an international rumpus:

Among the American manufactures were some fine soaps, and among these a small head, done in white Castile, and so exactly like marble that the Queen doubted the soap story, and in her impulsive, investigating way, was about to test it with a scratch of her shawl-pin when the Yankee exhibitor stayed her hand, and drew forth a courteous apology by a loyal remonstrance— 'Pardon, Your Majesty,—*it is the head of Washington*'.

These were happy times for Queen Victoria. An American visitor, seeing her open Parliament in State the year after the Exhibition, concluded 'I think I never saw anything sweeter than her smile of recognition, given to some of her friends in the gallery'. The following year, war clouds began to loom on the horizon. As a preliminary to the outbreak of the Crimean War wild rumours spread through London that Prince Albert was a Russian spy and about to be incarcerated in the Tower. Crowds assembled to see him, and possibly his wife, brought in through Traitors' Gate. Ballads were circulated to add colour to the rumours.

> Last Monday night, all in a fright,
>   Al out of bed did tumble.
> The German lad was raving mad.
>   How he did groan and grumble!
> He cried to Vic, 'I've cut my stick:
>   To St. Petersburg go right slap.'
> When Vic, 'tis said, jumped out of bed,
>   And whopped him with her night-cap.

All such stories were of course complete nonsense, and the hard work of the Queen and her husband in reviewing troops and visiting the wounded soon restored royal popularity. Although Victoria did not care for wars, she deferred to no-one in her admiration of bravery. She pressed forward with the institution of the Victoria Cross and, at her own suggestion, became the first Sovereign personally to present medals to the troops. Afterwards Lord Malmesbury recorded a remarkable conversation:

After the ceremony, Lady Seymour, whom I met, told me that Mrs. Norton, talking about it to Lord Panmure, asked, 'Was the Queen touched?'

'Bless my soul, no!' was the reply. 'She had a brass railing before her, and no one could touch her.'

Mrs. Norton then said, 'I mean, was she moved?'

'Moved!' answered Lord Panmure, 'she had no occasion to move!'

Mrs. Norton then gave up in despair.

Military reviews became quite the order of the day. There was

THE LAST YEARS WITH ALBERT

nothing the young Queen Victoria liked better than dressing up
in uniform, getting on horseback and reviewing her troops. (In
view of her interest it is surprising that it was not till her 70th
birthday that she witnessed what she called 'the Trooping of the
Colour, a very old ceremony . . . a beautiful sight, and one I believe I had never seen before'.) In the relatively unwashed days of
the 1850s close proximity to large numbers of men could have
disadvantages. Turning to Lord Palmerston at one review she held
a handkerchief to her nose and said, 'Don't you think there is
rather a . . .' 'Oh, that's what we call *esprit de corps*, Ma'am,' replied Pam, that irrepressible hangover from the Regency. Another
story which went the rounds was a cockney servant's account of
what the Queen said when meeting a troopship after the Battle of
Balaclava. She and Albert were taken aboard the wrong vessel and
found only four soldiers. 'Is this h'all H'Albert,' she is recounted
as saying, 'Gawd's truth! This 'ere's a bloody feeasco!'

During these years the Queen and Albert (officially created
Prince Consort in 1857) were carrying a heavy work load. As
Lord Clarendon discovered, 'one must be up *very early* to teach
this worthy family anything they don't know already'. When
Palmerston became Prime Minister his light-hearted reports
helped to make work a pleasure as well as a duty. Victoria was
particularly delighted with his anecdote about one of the Irish
Members of Parliament: 'It is said that Mr. Scully . . . observed to
a friend that the House of Commons is a strange assembly; that
when he first came into it he talked sense, and nobody listened to
him, but since he had taken to talking nonsense he had become a
favourite with the House.' She still did not always agree with
Palmerston. During the Indian Mutiny, for example, his Government was being criticised for its inactivity. 'The Queen has just
received Lord Palmerston's letter of yesterday,' she wrote, 'and
must say that if she had been in the House she would have joined
in saying that the Government were not doing enough . . .' 'It is
fortunate for those from whose opinions your Majesty differs,'
replied Pam, gallant as ever, 'that your Majesty is not in the House
of Commons, for they would have to encounter a formidable

antagonist in argument.' Certainly she had by now mastered the art of expressing herself forcefully. Indeed, there were occasions when she scarcely disguised the fact that she could hardly agree with the actions of even the Almighty. 'Thy will be done,' she grudgingly wrote on the death of Peel, 'but it does seem mysterious that in these troubled times . . . *he* . . . should be taken . . .'

The biggest family event of the 1850s was the marriage of the Princess Royal to Prince Frederick ("Fritz") of Prussia. Incurably romantic, Queen Victoria was overjoyed that this was a love-match like her own. As the wedding approached she became more nervous than the bride, so much so that the wedding-morning photograph of father, mother and daughter was blurred by the Queen's inability to keep still. Small wonder that, when she saw Wilson, the photographer, taking pictures of the landscape around Balmoral, she was moved to poke fun at herself: 'Good morning to you, Mr. Wilson. No pictures spoilt to-day, I trust. How nice to have a sitter like Lochnager who can't fidget about.' Nor could she fail to see the funny side of Albert leading a delegation of an organisation of which he was head to congratulate her on the marriage of their daughter: "It was very droll to hear Papa speaking to me of "all the virtues of H.R.H. the Princess Royal".'

Though the departure of the Princess for a new life in Berlin was accompanied by floods of tears, in some ways the change of status brought mother and daughter even closer together. 'I experience everything she feels,' the Queen boasted, 'and since I myself feel so young, our relationship is more like two sisters.' A lifelong correspondence ensued. On the mother's side at least it was completely uninhibited.

It is most odious [she was soon writing] that they have spread a report that you and I are both in what I call an unhappy condition! . . . All who love you hope that you will be spared this trial for a year yet, as you are so very young . . . If I had had a year of happy enjoyment with dear Papa, to myself—how thankful I should have been! But I was 3 years and $\frac{1}{2}$ older; therefore I was for it at once—and furious I was.

Nor was the Queen in her letters above poking fun at herself:

> Aldershot was really rather too hot a pleasure. Hazy—not a
> particle of wind and such a sickening sun—we all agreed it was
> no hotter in August. [It was March!] I have paid for it, though
> I did not ride and held a large parasol over my nose, by a
> scorched really sore red face, but I hope powder will prevent
> my being too great a figure at the levée.

Life at home went on as happily as ever. Increasingly now informality was preferred to formal entertainment. Some seasons,
though, were quite brilliant. The highlight during the Exhibition
year was a fancy-dress ball of the Restoration period. Gladstone
turned up as a judge of the High Court of Admiralty. In '56 a new
ballroom was added to Buckingham Palace, capable of meeting the
needs of the now well-established waltz. Sir Sidney Lee gives the
following as the Queen's dancing score over the next two months:

> On May 9 the new ballroom at Buckingham Palace, which
> Prince Albert has devised, was brought into use for the first
> time on the occasion of the Princess Royal's début. On May 27
> the Queen attended a ball at the Turkish Ambassador's, and to
> the Ambassador's embarrassment chose him for her partner in
> the first country dance.
>
> She was still regarded as one of the most graceful performers
> of the day in minuets and country dances. At a ball in the
> Waterloo Gallery at Windsor on June 10 she danced every
> dance, and finally performed a Scottish reel to the bagpipes. On
> June 26 the Duke of Westminster gave a great ball in her honour
> at Grosvenor House, where she equally distinguished herself.

The next year, when the Prussian general Von Moltke was in
London for the royal wedding, he was quite overwhelmed by the
gay round of royal social life, with visits to the theatre and Royal
Ascot and a State Ball at which 'the Queen danced with unabated
energy'.

There was much more dancing on a less formal basis—at
Osborne a 'morning dancing fête', at Windsor 'a gay dance and

two merry reels', at Buckingham Palace 'a dinner and dance (only about 30 people after dinner) in the Saloon, just as the one we had, when you dearest child, were still here . . . I hardly liked valsing thinking of you'. At Balmoral strenuous dancing was an integral part of life. All in all, Victoria was proud of her continued agility. 'We had a gay ball last night,' she wrote when she was forty-one, 'and I, old woman, danced a great deal, but I do so enjoy reels'. She was indeed quite athletic for her age. Her young cousin Mary Adelaide (who, admittedly, because of her enormous size, was probably not a very formidable opponent) was still in demand when the Queen was forty as her partner in games of shuttlecock and battledore.

Visits to the theatre were still made with great enthusiasm. 'We have been four times to the play this week,' runs one of her letters of 1860. The royal preference was still for the lighter side of things: 'The Princess Capricia, who cries pearls, was very amusing.' She was so taken with 'a pretty new piece called *The Babes in the Wood*' that she went back a second time. The melodrama *Colleen Bawn* had great appeal—'the scene when the poor Colleen is thrown into the water and all but drowned is wonderfully done'. Back she went to see it again, this time taking the Prince of Wales to share in the excitement.

It was, however, as her letters to the Princess Royal confirm, in the passive pleasures of family life that the Queen found the greatest contentment. Novel-reading still formed an important part of her life here and Albert appears to have shared her romantic tastes. Once Victoria confessed to her daughter that, though *Barchester Towers* was 'very amusing', 'I didn't like reading it aloud to Papa as there was not enough romance in it'. George Eliot measured up to the romantic requirements: 'Dear Papa was much amused and interested by Adam Bede, which I was delighted to read a second time.' Even the seduction of Hetty Victoria took in her stride. It was, after all, 'only a true picture of what constantly (and very naturally) happens'. Luckily, George Eliot was able to describe such things without committing the deadly sin of being 'coarse'.

9 'What I think would give Victoria great pleasure'—a children's fête at Coburg, 1845

10 Both seen and heard—the royal children with their parents

11 Victoria at thirty-five. 'I myself feel so young.'

Her own continuing naiveté as she approached middle age was obvious from the way she took to heart so much of what she read.

> I have finished *The Mill on the Floss* and must say it made a great impression on me. The writing and description of feelings is wonderful and painful! Why must they be drowned, but poor Philip Wakem I pity most of all! Stephen did behave very ill, Tom had much good, but was very hard.

Harriet Beecher Stowe discovered this same intense involvement when her anti-slavery novel *Dred* was published. She heard that the Queen had begun it 'the very minute she got it', and how 'she preferred it to *Uncle Tom's Cabin*, how interested she was in Nina, how provoked when she died, and how angry that something dreadful did not happen to Tom Gordon'.

Ceremonial life produced its own crop of amusing incidents. Eleanor Stanley reported on the farce which occurred during the visit of eccentric Victor Emmanuel of Sardinia:

> When he arrived I hear he did not understand he was to kiss his sister sovereign, so that the poor Queen stood putting up her cheek to him for ever so long before he condescended to touch it; however, he is said to have quite made up for this backwardness when she gave him the royal salute after investing him with the Garter, for after kissing her face he began upon her hand, and bestowed upon it three kisses that resounded round the room.
>
> The 'suite' were also amused, when he put out his leg for the Garter to be buckled on, he stuck out first one and then the other, and at last he said to the Queen in his loud, short voice, '*Laquelle?*' She nearly let fall the Garter for laughing, the Prince was in fits, and all the K.G.s at the table began to titter.

Perhaps the fault was not altogether on the King's side. When they came to the garter-investing part of the ceremony with Napoleon III, Lord Clarendon drily observed that the Queen 'fumbled ostensibly, as she always does, to show her unfamiliarity with the slightly indiscreet article of male attire'.

When Esterhazy, the Austrian general, came to Osborne he too was quite a handful.

> ... he arrived at 11 p.m. instead of for dinner ... His mode of apologising for this was slipping his hand up the Queen's sleeve and tickling her arm and he *kept amusing himself* in the same way all Monday to the infinite amusement of H.M. He took the breathe out of the body and dignity of the Consort by *hugging* him. H.R.H. made as rapid a retreat as circumstances permitted but was stopped by the pianoforte where Esterhazy recovered his advantage and held him tight by the waist ...

Coping with experiences like these no doubt helped Victoria to react with apparent equanimity to such absurdities as the visit of a delegation from Siam. For, as Clarendon confided to his wife, 'they crawled the whole length of the Throne Room on all fours with their noses to the floor, and the Queen boasted much to me afterwards of having kept her countenance'. Later contact with Siam was to prove equally disconcerting. One of her equerries once had the duty of asking a visiting Siamese princess to sign the Queen's birthday book. When he asked her when her birthday was she failed to understand him. So he said, 'On what day were you born?' Her reply was: 'On the ninth waxing of the moon of the season of Pyotto in the year San Yow.' The poor equerry thought for a moment and then asked her to sign her name on a blank sheet of paper. Lord Palmerston took pleasure in reporting the even more erratic behaviour of the ruler of Egypt when asked to sign his name in the Queen's book:

> Your Majesty may perhaps have heard that Ibrahim Pasha learned to write his name while your Majesty's messenger was waiting for the Queen's album; and that when he had written his name in the book he threw away the pen, saying that as the first time in his life that he had written his name had been for the Queen of England, so it should be the last, for he would never write it again for anyone else.

During these years what most impressed the more discerning

European visitors, able to compare the British Court with their own, was Queen Victoria's unaffected ease of manner. One minor German prince was much struck by it when he visited Buckingham Palace in '59: 'She spoke in a very sympathetic, unaffected and natural way to me (quite unlike the apathetic chatter of Continental Sovereigns) and enquired after all my family, showing her kindness of heart, of which I had heard much.' Another German, Baron Bunsen, commended her for not having 'the fixed mask only too common in the royal rank of society'. During a visit by the King of Prussia he watched her closely and gave her full marks. 'My impression of the Queen's deportment is that it is perfect in ease and dignity: she conversed eagerly with the King, laughing heartily (no *company* laugh) at the things he said to entertain her.'

So inclined was Queen Victoria to laugh that she sometimes found it an embarrassment. Certain people, Lord Granville for example, had a particularly diverting effect on her. Once, said Granville, she told him 'that she wished me to go with her to Ireland but that I must promise not to make her laugh at the wrong moments'. In some respects, though, Granville undervalued the Royal Family. 'Why bother,' he remarked, 'to tell your best stories in a house where you get far louder laughter by shutting your thumb in the door?' There certainly was this slapstick element in the Queen's sense of humour, but this was by no means the whole story. Later she was to tell Disraeli that the part of *Endymion* which amused her was the episode when the Athanasian Creed was discussed—hardly a matter of shutting one's thumb in the door. Granville might also have been surprised to learn of the subtle enjoyment she secretly obtained by inviting to Court 'a funny collection of antagonistic elements', i.e. politicians who were at loggerheads with one another—'The Happy Family, I call it'.

Again, it is easy to underestimate the extent of the Prince Consort's sense of humour. Even in these later years, when he was tired and overworked, it still broke through, particularly within the family circle. Victoria loved reporting his little quips to her daughter in Berlin. There was his comment on the Queen of

Naples, who was such an excellent shot: 'Pity she doesn't shoot
Garibaldi—Papa says.' When some pompous Prussians came to
Court they were 'so wonderfully absurd—that really one can't
help laughing at everything they say; Papa takes them off so well'.
He was equally capable of poking fun at his own family. 'Papa
is too naughty—when he read your letter saying that the poor
Queen envied your being able to cry he said "That you must be
very happy as you did it so easily! and that Lenchen ought to be
sent specially for the purpose".' He made play of his wife's proneness to feel sorry for herself during his infrequent absences. 'You
will be feeling,' he wrote in one letter, 'somewhat lonely and fore-
saken among the two and a half million human beings in London.'
The same jocularity was apparent after the birth of their last child,
Princess Beatrice: 'Baby practises her scales like a good *prima donna*
before a performance.' But his wife was like a caged lion: 'Victoria
counts the hours and minutes like a prisoner.'

Beatrice proved to be extremely high-spirited and a great
source of pleasure to parents now approaching middle age.
'Princess Beatrice,' one of the Court recounted, 'had her little
supper with us all, and between whiles enlivened us with little bits
of poetry, "Twinkle, twinkle," "Little Miss Muffet," "Humpty
Dumpty", and several others, speaking remarkably plainly and
nicely, but showing a considerable degree of character in her choice
of poems and her claiming of the rewards (biscuits) for repeating
them.' Only a year after her arrival the royal couple learned from
Berlin that they were shortly to become grandparents. In spite of
the reservations she had expressed about early pregnancies the
Queen could not conceal her excitement from her daughter:

I delight in the idea of being a grandmama; to be that at 39
(D.V.) and to look and feel young is great fun, only I wish I
could go through it for you, dear, and save you all the annoyance. But that can't be helped. I think of my next birthday
being spent with my children and grandchild. It will be a treat.

Much advice is lavished on the expectant mother, even down to
the sending of special stays with precise instructions on how to

wear them. After the birth of a boy—the future Kaiser William II—the Queen extracted the maximum enjoyment from her new status. 'There were such quantities of people out on Thursday when we went to open Parliament,' she told her daughter, 'and so enthusiastic—all to see Grandpapa and Grandmama.' Albert was even more delighted the following year with the arrival of a granddaughter.

> Little girls are much prettier than boys. I advise her to model herself on Aunt Beatrice. That excellent lady has not a moment to spare. 'I have no time,' she says when asked for anything, 'I must write letters to my niece.'

Surrounded by her family and her husband's loving care, Queen Victoria felt secure and contented. On her twenty-first wedding anniversary she gave thanks that Albert still showed her 'the same tender love of the very first days of our marriage'. Lord Torrington, by no means the Prince Consort's greatest admirer, had to confess that he was 'most agreeably surprised and pleased' at the happiness and informality that was so evident in the Royal Family's Christmas of 1860.

> I have never seen a much more agreeable sight. It was royalty putting aside its state and becoming in words, acts and deeds one of ourselves—no forms and not a vestige of ceremony. Even as in a public bazaar, where people jostle one another, so lords, grooms, Queen and princes laughed and talked, forgot to bow, and freely turned their backs on one another. I have never seen more real happiness.

This was to be the Prince Consort's last Christmas. On December 14th 1861 he died at the age of forty-two. At one blow Queen Victoria's safe, contented existence was shattered.

CHAPTER IX

The First Rays of Sunshine

How I, who leant on him for all and everything—without whom I did nothing, moved not a finger, not a print or photograph, didn't put on a gown or bonnet if he didn't approve, shall be able to go on, to live, to move, to help myself at difficult moments . . .

It was thus that a heartbroken Queen Victoria contemplated widowhood. The Princess Royal saw her mother's predicament in equally simple terms: 'Poor Mama has to go to bed and has to get up alone—for ever.' She looked, the Princess thought, 'so young and pretty with her white cap and widow's weeds'. 'So young and innocent with it all,' agreed Augusta Bruce. 'Somehow the Queen looked like a child,' echoed the Duchess of Atholl.

And essentially the Queen's mental outlook was still childlike and simple. Emotionally she was more akin to a peasant woman than a woman-of-the-world. It was not for nothing that she felt more at home with cottagers and servants than with sophisticated people. Leonid Vladimirov's description of the Russian peasant mentality could equally well be applied to her:

> The Russian's feelings are close to the surface. . . . Subjected to such sudden emotional pressures as excess of joy or anguish, the Russian does not dream of hiding his feelings . . . The outburst may serve at times as a safety valve, releasing pressures that, left to accumulate, might produce damage . . .

So it was that Queen Victoria gave full vent to her grief, and that eventually the sunny side of her nature again began to break through the gloom. First an amusing episode would momentarily divert her, then she began to have bouts of cheerfulness, till in time her robust ability to enjoy life fully reasserted itself. That her own brand of common sense never deserted her is only too evident from her reaction to the divine who suggested that she should henceforth regard herself as married to Christ—'*That is what I call twaddle!*' Only weeks after the Prince's death she was writing a detailed account of their daily life together, down to quite intimate details. 'He slept in long white drawers, which enclosed his feet as well as his legs, like the sleeping suits worn by small babies . . . Poor darling little Beatrice used to be so delighted to see him dress and when she arrived and he was dressed she made dearest Albert laugh so, by saying "What a pity"!'

It was Beatrice's playful ways which now helped make her mother's life less gloomy during the first dark months of widowhood. 'Baby,' said Augusta Bruce, was 'enchanting and bewitching':

> The Queen says 'Baby mustn't have it, it's not good for baby.' 'But she likes it, my dear' is the reply as she helps herself . . .
>
> Princess Beatrice was 'notty' with her Mama at luncheon and Thurston was summoned to take her away. When T. appeared she appealed to her with wounded dignity and feelings: 'It was only for her (the Queen) I came downstairs.' 'Such base ingratitude.'

'What a pity it is,' she remarked to her mother one day, 'that I was too little to be at your marriage.' She was not above playing practical jokes. One day she was in the room where the Queen, wearing an apron as was her habit, was working on State papers. Silently Beatrice tied the apron strings to the back of the chair so that after the child had gone the Queen found she could not move. Another time, 'Baby's fidgetyness was beyond everything, and she ended up by throwing all the milk over herself.' There was further amusement at the Prince of Wales' wedding. Beatrice, not quite six, was taken round Windsor to see the decorations. She was shocked by what caught her eye. 'She never thought there was *stays* in shops.'

At this wedding the Queen's grandson, William, was also in evidence, though he did not cover himself in glory. Not only did he call his grandmama 'Duck' but he threw his aunt's muff out of the carriage window. During the marriage service he took several bites out of the leg of one of his young kilted uncles. At other times, however, his mother, encouraged by the example of young Beatrice, found him a fruitful source of anecdotes to amuse the Queen.

> He has a sergeant who comes in the morning to make him do exercises, in order that he should be made to hold himself upright and use his left arm. When he does not wish to do his exercises he begins to say his prayers and bits of poetry, and the other day he asked the man, before Sophie Dubeneck who was shocked, 'Do you put a nightgown on when you undress yourself and go to bed?'

The Queen was not shocked. 'What you tell me about William's sayings,' she replied appreciatively, 'are too delightful.'

It became clear, too, that she still obtained considerable pleasure from the unusual and the bizarre.

> Princess Alice [Gladstone told his wife from Balmoral] has got a black boy here who was given to her, and he produces a great sensation on Deeside, where the people never saw anything of the kind and cannot conceive it. A woman, and an intelligent one, cried out in amazement on seeing him, and said she would certainly have fallen down but for the Queen's presence. She said nothing would induce her to wash his clothes *as the black would come off*! This story the Queen told me in good spirits.

When Siamese twins appeared on the London scene Victoria was fascinated. 'I send you,' runs one of her letters to her daughter, 'a curious photo of the Siamese twins (very horrid they look) for you to look at, which I beg back.' She was also struck by the in-

THE FIRST RAYS OF SUNSHINE

congruity of some Maori chiefs who came to Osborne. 'They were half in native, half in European dress,' she observed. 'The women wore silk petticoats with their strange cloaks of matting and feathers in their hair.' It would be interesting to know what the Maoris thought of Queen Victoria.

In time more subtle subjects of conversation again began to provide her with enjoyment. 'There was,' reported a new Maid of Honour, 'much more conversation than I had expected; the Queen talking and laughing cheerfully. She and the Dean spoke about sermons and Presbyterian preachers; and the Dean made no bones of making occasional hits at the Scotch reverences, which the Queen took as a good joke.' A visiting German professor discovered that her worship of the Prince Consort did not extend to his tiresome brother. Indeed, 'with womanly wit and womanly penetration she made unsparing merriment over the Duke, his variable quixotic disposition'. More amusing company than most was Landseer the painter. 'The Queen, in high force, talked all dinner time, and was highly amused at Landseer's anecdotes about his animals etc.' During a stay at Balmoral she was herself persuaded to take up her artistic interests again, though the extraordinary way she chose to do this, according to one of those present, shows that a certain degree of eccentricity now characterised her behaviour.

> When the place selected for sketching was reached, the Queen seated herself in the middle of the country-road, with a round stone from the Dee as a rest for her paint-box, Lady Churchill holding an umbrella to shade the Queen's eyes. Princess Louise sat on a stone a little farther away, while Mr. Leitch attended the party as instructor, and John Brown looked after the pony. The country folk stared in astonishment as they passed by, and Her Majesty heartily enjoyed the fun, and seemed to revive a little of her lost animation.

London and official functions were for long avoided at all costs. At length a wag posted a notice outside Buckingham Palace: 'These commanding premises to be sold, in consequence of the late occupant's declining business.' (Labouchere was later to suggest it be used to accommodate fallen woman.) Victoria's taste for country life, which had developed during Albert's lifetime, now became a positive mania. 'As the years went on indeed,' wrote General Grey in his *Life of the Prince Consort*, 'this preference for the country on the part of the Queen grew stronger and stronger, till residence in London became positively distasteful to her.' To this statement she added a note in the strange English to which she was sometimes prone: 'It was also injurious to her health, as she suffered much from the extreme weight and thickness of the atmosphere, which gave her the headache.' Gone for ever were those halycon days when Victoria had loved Buckingham Palace and the Regent's Park was 'quite country enough' for her. But the change was not entirely in her imagination. London really had changed for the worse during those 25 years. In addition to the pollution from smoke, the countryside was far less accessible. 'And alas! any quiet and comparatively country drives, which I took formerly, are gone—for streets extend in every possible direction and make it most unpleasant.' But in the 1860s she introduced one new feature to the London scene, the Buckingham Palace Garden Party. The first seems to have been an incongrous affair. Though not beginning till 4.30 in the afternoon, it was given the old-fashioned title of 'Breakfast'. The prescribed dress for men was accordingly morning trousers with evening coats.

It was in London too that Queen Victoria sampled what was for her a unique literary gathering. It was arranged by the Dean of Westminster; and the Grotes, the Lyells, Carlyle and Browning were present. This was shortly after the Queen had published her first book, *Leaves from a Journal of Our Life in the Highlands.* 'Rather amusing the literary line the Queen has taken up,' thought Mary Bulteel, the Maid of Honour who married Henry Ponsonby. But, though Victoria was pleased at the popularity of her book, she had no illusions about her literary abilities. She made this clear when she met Dickens. She had been an admirer of his since those early days when (in spite of the disapproval of her mother and Lord

Melbourne) she had so enjoyed *Oliver Twist* but did not meet him until shortly before his death. She thought him 'very agreeable'. 'He talked about his latest works, of America, the strangeness of the people there, of the division of classes in England, which he hoped would get better in time.' He had, she decided, 'a large, loving mind'. Then, to set their relationship in perspective, she presented him with a copy of her book inscribed 'From the humblest of writers to one of the greatest'.

Dickens no doubt avoided telling her of his infatuation in his younger days. At the time of her marriage he had imagined himself violently in love with her. 'I am sorry to say,' he had confided to a friend, 'I have fallen hopelessly in love with the Queen, and wander up and down with vague and dismal thoughts of running away with a maid of honour.' He had not been alone in his passion: scores of young men—courtiers, businessmen, men-about-town— had been carried away by similar romantic feelings for her in those happy, far-off days.

The widowed Queen's experiment of meeting writers in a group was never repeated. It was not her style. Henry Ponsonby, when he became her Private Secretary, understood her feelings:

> Explaining why the Queen preferred the company of Mrs. Grant, the wife of the Head Keeper, to that of Mrs. Grote, the wife of the historian, Colonel Ponsonby asserted, 'Mrs. Grant speaks of her children and the tea cakes and scones. These require no preparation. But Mrs. Grote might suddenly ask whether she approved of female doctors.'

Queen Victoria was incapable of dissimulation. The honest answer she would have had to give Mrs. Grote's question would have been 'No'. For one thing, she had a violent dislike, strange in a female Sovereign, of what she called 'this mad folly of women's rights'. Furthermore, her squeamishness about 'the animal side of our nature' made her profoundly shocked at the very idea of 'allowing *young girls* and young men to enter the dissecting room together'.

She did approve of women novelists. Charlotte Brontë—

capable of writing so passionately without involving the animal side at all—she admired greatly.

> Finished *Jane Eyre* which is really a wonderful book, very peculiar in parts, but so powerfully and admirably written, such a fine tone in it, such fine religious feeling, and such beautiful writing. The description of the mysterious maniac's nightly appearance awfully thrilling, Mr. Rochester's character a very remarkable one, and Jane Eyre's herself a beautiful one.

Later Marie Corelli became a great favourite, though the Princess Royal (by this time the Empress Frederick) did not agree with her mother's assessment of that popular novelist. During a right royal argument on the subject Fritz Ponsonby, as he later confessed, dropped a gigantic brick:

> The Queen said she would rank as one of the greatest writers of the time, while the Empress thought her writings were trash. I was seated at the other end of the large dining-room table and therefore had not, unfortunately, heard the commencement of the discussion. The Empress suddenly called across the table to me and asked me what I thought of Marie Corelli. Quite unconscious of the fact that the Queen was an admirer of this authoress, I replied that her books undoubtedly had a large sale, but that I thought the secret of her popularity was that her writings appealed to the semi-educated. Whereupon the Empress clapped her hands, and the subject dropped with alarming suddenness.

Unfortunately, according to Lord Redesdale, even the Queen's appreciation of books of more lasting worth, such as *Alice in Wonderland*, could lead her into trouble:

> Queen Victoria, it seems, was so much struck by *Alice* that she commanded Sir Henry Ponsonby to write and compliment the author, adding she would be greatly pleased to receive any other book of his. He was greatly flattered and sent her his *Syllabus of Plane Algebraical Geometry*.

Although the Queen soon got back into her habit of reading novels, it was from poetry that she derived her keenest pleasure during early widowhood. 'Poems I am fond of in all shapes.' She had given up going to the theatre but quickly made use of Lady Martin's talents as a former actress to make her readings as dramatic as possible. Lady Martin confided to a friend, 'H.M. admires Mrs. Browning immensely, but oddly, she does not care for Mr. Browning—says she cannot understand him.' With Tennyson she struck up a life-long friendship. Not only did his poetry greatly appeal to her, but Tennyson the man attracted her. He behaved in a perfectly natural and down-to-earth manner, treating her not so much as a queen as a 'dear and honoured lady'. His very bluntness could be amusing. Visiting her at Osborne he told her he was much bothered at his home by intruders. 'She said she was not much troubled here,' his wife records, which brought from Tennyson a typically forthright answer: 'Perhaps I should not be either if I could stick a sentry at my gates.' When he paid her a left-handed compliment by saying that the trees on her estate would be pretty in thirty years time, he was rewarded with a broad smile.

So very gradually she broadened her life-style. In 1866 she attended a dance at Windsor for the first time in nearly five years, 'looking on with real amusement'. Two years later she made the first of the pleasure jaunts abroad that she was to enjoy for the rest of her life. She stayed at the Pension Wallace in Lucerne. Here it was that Henry Ponsonby proved that she still had her old belly-laugh. One evening at dinner the royal physician, Dr. Jenner, was describing his expedition up the mountains in the company of an exceedingly plain German governess. Ponsonby, who had a gift for provoking laughter, then joined in the conversation.

I simply asked what the tourists thought of their relationship. He replied 'Oh, of course they thought she was Madame' which created some laughter. Then he added 'The guide was very decided and made us give up the horses we rode up and come down in a chair.'

'What?' I asked. 'Both in one chair?' Well, there was nothing odd in this—but everyone laughed. I turned to Miss Bids. She was purple. On the other side I tried to speak to Princess Louise. She was choking. I looked across to Jenner. He was convulsed. Of course this was too much. I gave way; we all had a *fou rire* till the tears ran down my cheeks which set off the Queen. I never saw her laugh so much. She said afterwards it was my face.

Her broad sense of humour had remained intact. Once again members of her Household found it rewarding to save up amusing, even risqué, stories for her consumption. As Patricia Lindsay knew, no-one was more successful at this than the Duchess of Atholl.

I have often heard my father speak of the Queen's intense amusement on one occasion when he was present and the Duchess told the story of the comical advertisement regarding the Dunkeld and Blairgowrie coach, which was once posted in the village of Dunkeld. The coach was named 'The Duchess of Atholl' and the inn from which it started was the 'Duke's Arms'. The notice ran as follows: 'The Duchess of Atholl leaves the Duke's Arms every lawful morning at six o'clock.'

CHAPTER X

Highland Charm

This solitude, the romance and wild loveliness of everything here, the absence of hotels and beggars, the independent simple people, who all speak Gaelic here, all make beloved Scotland the proudest, finest country in the world.

This tribute, written by Queen Victoria during a visit to Invertrossachs, sums up the charm which the Highlands increasingly held for her. There, more than ever during her widowhood, she escaped whenever she could. The quiet and the natural beauty acted as a tonic for her nerves, and, as Patricia Lindsay knew, the ease of manner of the people was a perpetual refreshment to her.

The freedom of their homely speech interested and amused her, for she knew well that no disrespect was meant, as when one old woman would welcome her with an invitation 'Come awa ben sit doon, Queen Victoria,' or another 'Is this you, my Sovereign?'

On one of her longer excursions she once met and conversed with an old woman who did not recognise her until a lady-in-waiting told her it was the Queen, when the old lady dropped her knitting, seized Her Majesty's hands, and exclaimed 'What! —the Queen! Happy and glorious, long to reign over us!'—a speech which gave great amusement and pleasure to her audience.

Straight speaking and informal behaviour pleased her when

others more haughty would have taken offence. After she had been taught to spin by an old Highland woman she took it as a great compliment when the gillie Grant told her, at the age of forty-six, 'Ye spin as well as any old woman in the country'. She was just as happy to admit that knitting was certainly not her forte:

> ... she acknowledges herself, with a hearty laugh, the justice of a remark made by an old peasant woman, who, unaware of the Queen's personality, picked up a scrap of knitting that Her Majesty had done, and curtly observed that she pitied the 'gude mon' if he got no better made stockings that that.

The peasant in her own mental make-up made her feel at ease with such people. In some ways she longed to be more like them. 'The Queen,' bemoaned one of her Household, 'will talk as if she were Mrs. Jones and might live just where she liked.' It was noticed, by Patricia Lindsay among others, that she also had the peasant's ability to be moved easily from sorrow to laughter:

> I shall never forget the gentle, womanly kindness of the Queen on one occasion when ... she paid a special visit of sympathy to my poor mother, who, though recognising her august guest, was unable to speak, or even rise from her chair to receive her. An amusing incident, I remember relieved the sadness of the visit, and afforded Her Majesty a hearty laugh. A little nephew about three years old was with us, and had on a pair of red shoes, of which he was not a little proud. He at once called attention to them, asking 'Do you like my pretty new shoes? I got them because the Queen was coming.'

Victoria was no less keen than the local people to uphold the Highland traditions:

> The Queen always enjoyed seeing people happy, and encouraged the keeping up of all the old Highland customs, such as the torchlight dance of the keepers and gillies when the stags were brought home after a good day's stalking. Weirdly picturesque scenes these dances were, held in front of the castle,

12 John Brown in 1860, 'the perfection of a servant . . . He thinks of everything.'

13 The new ballroom at Buckingham Palace. 'My Terpsichorean feelings are pretty strong.'

14 Drama at Windsor: the most active royal interest in the theatre since Charles II

with the hills and woods and the figures of the men fitfully lit up by the light of the blazing pine torches.

The old customs belonging to Hallow'een always interested the Queen and she desired that they should be fully carried out when at Balmoral. Consequently fires blazed on many of the hills, and lighted torches called 'sownachs' were borne round the bounds of the various farms and housesteads to keep off the evil spirits supposed to be let loose on All Hallows' Eve.

The proper forms were observed when she took possession of the new house she had had built for herself at the Glasshalt Shiel. At a house-warming she found it relaxing to sit with the servants watching a 'merry pretty little ball' consisting of 'five animated reels', and when her newly-married cousin Mary Adelaide arrived at the Castle she was given the traditional torch-lit reception. A wild dance followed together with a spectacle rather less typical of the Scottish Highlands—'a grand performance of Christy Minstrels'.

One festivity to which Queen Victoria was incurably addicted was known as 'the gillies' ball'. Attendance here enabled her to combine very neatly her respect for tradition, her desire to associate with simple country folk, and her old love of dancing. She herself started dancing again at these functions long before more formal dancing was thought of. The Royal Household did not share her enthusiasm. They considered them rowdy affairs. Moreover they were often held in the open air in the foulest weather when over-indulgence in alcohol was the only protection against the cold. Just after the Balmoral factor died Henry Ponsonby reported 'much low spirit in the household at the announcement of another gillies' ball'. By curious royal reasoning mourning was not allowed to interfere with this hallowed tradition. 'It is not put off,' Ponsonby explained, 'as the Queen does not regard it as gaiety, and in this the household heartily concur.' Once, when she was in her sixties and had excused herself from holding an official levée, they were quick to point out that 'she remained at a Ball at Balmoral last autumn from 10 to 12 and danced at it repeatedly'.

Another time Ponsonby slipped away from the gillies' revels. He was missed, so that on his return 'explanations ensued, culminating in my dancing a Hooligan with the Queen'.

On traditional occasions at Balmoral it was customary for excessive drinking to take place among the servants. To this Queen Victoria (who normally prided herself on knowing pretty well everything that went on around her) turned a completely blind eye. The fact that alcohol had been so much part of things in the Prince's day no doubt encouraged her in her attitude. Though Albert himself had been abstemious he had, on his own confession, after hearing the news of the fall of Sebastopol joined in 'a veritable witch's dance, supported by whisky'. The Queen, who would resort to euphemisms when it suited her, described the same scene as 'wild and exciting beyond everything' and the participants 'in great ecstasy'. She was to be equally reticent when her carriage overturned and 'we were all precipitated to the ground'. Though she received a black eye all she would say about the coachman was that he was 'utterly confused and bewildered'. Yet liquor oozes from every word. John Brown, too, was a heavy drinker. Whenever he was worse for wear Victoria described him as 'unwell' and quickly drew a heavy veil over the subject. It is said that on one occasion, Brown having actually crashed to the ground in a drunken stupor, the Queen tried to cover up by declaring 'she had distinctly been aware of a slight earthquake shock'. But then Victoria had a curious conception of earthquakes. Once, at midnight in the south of France, she thought she detected 'the regular rumblings of an earthquake', only to be told that it was Sir Henry Ponsonby snoring in the room below.

'Bacchanalian' was the description given by Frederick (Fritz) Ponsonby, Sir Henry's son, to the atmosphere at a gillies' ball given in the latter part of the reign. Servants at the royal dinner table would be in 'hilarious' mood, spilling wine over both table and guests to the accompaniment of crockery crashing in the background. Victoria pretended not to notice.

The Queen had been brought up to think that everything was

excusable on the night of the Gillies' Ball, and that it was up to her to keep the conversation going so that no one would remark anything. She was most amusing and told stories that were really quite funny.

Yet, typically, Queen Victoria did not approve of over-indulgence among the upper classes. Lord Fife, her neighbour at Mar Lodge, was one who placed a somewhat excessive emphasis on alcohol—though once she thought he had reformed.

When Queen Victoria visited Mar Lodge one day, he said, 'I am sure Your Majesty will be pleased to hear that I have given up drinking brandy and soda water'. H.M., though no doubt a little taken aback, replied, 'I am indeed glad, Lord Fife. It will be so much better for your health'. Fife, however, continued, 'It is not a matter of my health, Your Majesty, I have found a much better drink—that is whisky and Apollinaris water, and I strongly recommend Your Majesty to try it'.

Curiously enough, it seems she did try it as some years later one of her attendants revealed, 'She has for many years contented herself with a small portion of Scotch whisky, which is distilled expressly for her near Balmoral, at the small distillery of John Begg, and which is carefully mixed by her personal attendant with either Apollinaris, soda or lithia water.' In spite of this rumours spread that she was a heavy drinker. Her granddaughter, Lady Milford Haven, has given one explanation for such stories:

Having suffered very severely from gout between the age of 45 and 60—once at Balmoral she had gout in both hands—the doctors had forbidden her to take any wine and she only drank whisky and water at her meals. The whisky, probably was finished by her servants and thence the legend has arisen of her drinking lots of alcohol.

What Fritz Ponsonby tells us of the Balmoral servants helps confirm this theory. Their whisky consumption, he says, 'was truly stupendous'. 'A drunken man,' asserts Ponsonby, 'was so common that no one ever remarked on it.'

Before my day there were what was called 'larders'. The stags that had been shot during the day were taken from the larders and placed in a row and all the gillies carried torches. The Queen came out after dinner and dancing took place, all of which was very pretty, but after she left it became an orgy of drink.

Another occasion when whisky ran freely was on the anniversary of the Prince Consort's birthday. All the stalkers, gillies, and people on the estate were expected to attend dressed in top-hats (what the people called a funeral hat) and black coats. A prayer was said in front of the Prince Consort's statue, and the Queen drove there in her carriage with two grey horses and an outrider. Then whisky was sent out as light refreshment at the back of the wood. The result was that the whole community was three parts intoxicated and when we went for a walk in the afternoon it was no uncommon sight to find a man in a top-hat and frockcoat fast asleep in the woods.

The result of all this was a curious reversal of roles. When that worldly gourmet Edward VII came to the throne he found it necessary to institute thorough-going reforms to stamp out the excessive drinking his supposedly strait-laced mother had made no effort to curb.

If Queen Victoria's own drinking was restricted, it certainly appears that she had a hearty appetite. When she resumed the practice of making long trips round the Highlands she was particularly impressed by the hospitality offered her by the Duchess of Atholl at Dunkeld:

> Excellent breakfasts, such splendid cream and butter! The Duchess has a very good cook, a Scotchwoman, and I thought how dear Albert would have liked it all. He always said things tasted better in smaller houses. There were several Scotch dishes, two soups, and the celebrated 'haggis' which I tried last night, and really liked very much.

It is small wonder that, according to Gladstone, she weighed eleven stone eight pounds, 'rather much for her height'.

Even without Albert these Highland trips, packed with simple incidents and beautiful scenery, gave her great pleasure. Arriving once at Dunrobin the Queen spotted a local character—'There was a most excited station-master who would not leave the crowd of poor country-people in quiet, but told them to "cheer again," another "cheer", etc., without ceasing.' At Dunrobin Castle there was further cause for mirth: 'The Duchess told Brown to open the sitting-room; and we found it occupied by a policeman in bed, which we were not at all prepared for, and which caused much amusement.' On her return journey her sense of the incongruous again came into play:

> Beatrice, Jane, and I got into a hired (not very beautiful) open landau . . . We were escorted by the 7th Dragoon Guards, which was thought better on account of the great crowds in Inverness, where no sovereign has been since my poor ancestress Queen Mary. This mixture of half state and humble travelling (we being in our common travelling dresses) was rather amusing.

Sometimes her Journal entries show that, 'Queen's English' or no, Queen Victoria was not immune to the Scottish dialect. During a trip to Inverlochy she observed 'there were little fields, fuller of weeds than corn, much laid by the wet, and frequently a "calvie" or "coo" of the true shaggy Highland character was actually feeding in them'. And Lady Lytton heard her lapsing into dialect in conversation with the servants:

> We stopped at a cottage to see a stout 'Maggie'. 'Have you got any money?' said the Queen to the Scotch servant . . .
> 'Aboot twelve shillings.'
> 'Ah, that won't do *at all*, I always give her five poond', answered the Queen with the Scotch accent.

Occasionally a Scottish phrase would be used for more important purposes. When her grandson, the Kaiser, was more than usually provocative, her reaction was to say he needed 'a good skelping'.

When she published her second book, *More Leaves from a Journal of a Life in the Highlands* dealing with her middle age in this Highland setting, it was noticed that the illustrations in it were not of royalty or courtiers but of servants and dogs. The dogs featured prominently in the text. Clearly the young Victoria's devotion to Dash was perpetuated in the widow's affection for Sharp and Noble. Sharp, 'a favourite collie of mine', was extremely high-spirited but prone, in the Queen's words, to occasional 'collie shangies'. (For her ignorant Sassanach readers the thoughtful authoress added a footnote. Shangies, she explained, was 'a Scotch word for quarrels or "rows" but taken from fights between collies'.) Noble was a more peaceable creature.

> My favourite collie Noble is always downstairs when we take our meals, and was so good, Brown making him lie down on a chair or couch, and he never attempted to come down without permission, and even held a piece of cake in his mouth without eating it, till told he might. He is the most 'biddable' dog I ever saw, and so affectionate and kind; if he thinks you are not pleased with him, he puts out his paw and begs in such an affectionate way.

As she grew older and was held in ever-increasing awe by human beings her attachment owed something to the saying of Schopen-hauer she was fond of quoting: 'If it were not for the honest faces of dogs we should forget the existence of sincerity.' Her interest led to some strange items appearing in the Court Circular. 'Lord Lurgan's famous champion Irish greyhound has had the honour of being presented to her Majesty,' the astonished world read on one occasion. 'Madam Hazer has had the honour of exhibiting her dog Minos before the Queen and the Royal Family,' runs another report, 'and her Majesty was very pleased with the performance.' Once again this was a throwback to the early days of the Queen's marriage when a 'learned horse' and 'an exceptionally great dog' were honoured visitors to Court.

With Court Circulars being issued on such subjects, it is not surprising that parodies began to appear. *Punch* published its own version in 1866:

Mr. John Brown walked on the slopes.

He subsequently partook of a haggis.

In the evening *Mr. John Brown* was pleased to listen to a bagpipe.

Mr. John Brown retired early.

The Queen's own two books on her life in the Highlands were, of course, sitting ducks for those inclined to poke fun. 'Not a book to leave lying about in the drawing room,' joked *The Spectator* in an imaginary review of the first volume, 'nor one to place indiscriminately in the hands of young men and maidens.' 'The trait that seems to be most prominent in Her Majesty's book,' commented *Punch*, 'is the tea tray.' Americans had even greater fun when the second volume appeared. A parody, entitled *John Brown's Legs or Leaves from a Journal in the Lowlands*, was brought out, dedicated to 'the memory of those extraordinary legs, poor scratched darlings'. The Queen's somewhat pedestrian existence and simple pleasures were ridiculed, with Brown's little attentions figuring prominently.

> Brown pushed me (in the hand-carriage) up quite a hill and then ran me down again. He did this several times and we enjoyed it very much . . . He then put me in a boat on the lake and rocked me for about half an hour. It was very exhilarating.

The Queen's style of writing, with its peculiar phraseology and emphatic underlinings, was, to say the least, highly individualistic. 'Such bad vulgar English,' declared her scandalised old aunt, the Duchess of Cambridge. The Queen herself knew of its shortcomings, and Lord John Russell had confirmed her in her opinion. She once told him 'how tiresome it was sometimes in writing, when one got into the middle of a long sentence from which one could not extricate oneself', adding in her naïve way, 'I often do so'. 'Yes, Ma'am, so I perceive,' came the honest answer. Nevertheless she refused to alter her style for publication, thus making herself a ready target for parody. Max Beerbohm, for one, became adept at the art. He even went to the trouble of inscribing his own copy of *More Leaves* with the words, 'For Mr. Beerbohm, the never-sufficiently-to-be-studied writer whom Albert looks down on affectionately I am sure—From his Sovereign Victoria R.I. Balmoral, 1898'. And in the same volume, beneath the engraving of Sharp, the collie, he inserted 'Such a dear, faithful noble *friend* and companion, and for whom Albert had the *greatest* respect also. Victoria R.I.'

Max Beerbohm could be a fearless deflator of royalty, as his cartoons of Edward VII were to show. But as his biographer David Cecil points out, Max was 'at his best making fun of somebody he liked'.

He did like the Queen. Sir Theodore Martin in his biography of Prince Albert speaks of her as 'the Great and the Good'. Max wrote in the margin 'or at any rate the Good and Human, the Likeable, the ever Lovable; and the Peculiar, the never Uninteresting'.

An enviable epitaph!

CHAPTER XI

Man Appeal

'I am,' Queen Victoria readily admitted, 'a person who has to cling to someone in order to find peace and comfort.' Without a doubt the greatest gift of the Highlands towards her peace and comfort was John Brown. 'God knows how much I want to be taken care of' was another of her *cris-de-coeur*. It was the care taken by Brown after Albert's death that transformed him from a mere gillie into 'my devoted attendant and friend'. Any suggestion, however, that they were married, or had an improper sexual relationship can be dismissed out of hand. Of Brown's 'usefulness' (her word again) there can be no doubt, but it was as a father-substitute rather than a husband-substitute.

Bluntness and directness were the secret of his success. The Queen knew she could rely on a straight answer, even if it were expressed in a brusque fashion. If anything the brusqueness gave the advice added appeal to her. Not so to members of her Household most of whom fiercely resented Brown's manner. Fritz Ponsonby quotes one example of the technique that roused their wrath:

> General Sir Lyndoch Gardiner, one of the Queen's Equerries, was one of Brown's pet aversions, although he was quite unconscious of the fact . . . On one occasion he came into waiting and on meeting Brown he enquired how the Queen was and what she had been doing lately. Brown replied, 'The Queen's very well. It was only the other day she said to me "There's that dommed old fool General Gardiner coming into waiting

and I know he'll be putting his bloody nose into everything that doesn't concern him".'

'History,' adds Ponsonby, 'does not relate what General Gardiner replied.'

That Brown was in the habit of translating the Queen's remarks into his own brand of uninhibited English is confirmed from other sources. The nervous official in charge of train journeys to Balmoral admitted to being the recipient of such 'royal' messages.

> Passing along the platform in the dead of night at Wigan, where usually nothing is heard or seen of Royal Travellers, I was surprised to find John Brown; and enquiring whether all was right, heard to my surprise 'No! The Queen says the carriage is shaking like the devil!'—a startling communication!

On another journey an overheated axle gave off a foul smell. 'The Queen wants to know. "What gars this stink?" is John Brown's remark as we pass along the platform.' Brown appears to have followed good precedents for misusing the Queen's name. Her cousin, the second Duke of Cambridge, for many years Commander-in-Chief, is said to have quoted her in front of the troops when violently denouncing the practice of swearing in the army: 'I was talking it over with the Queen last night and Her Majesty says she will be damned if she will have it.'

Victoria on her part, says Fritz Ponsonby, took delight in quoting—or misquoting—some of Brown's more colourful remarks.

> The Queen often quoted John Brown and seemed amused by his quaint expressions. At one time the Duchess of Roxburghe and Miss Stopford were not on speaking terms and when Miss Stopford was ill Sir James Reid, the Queen's doctor, suggested perhaps the Duchess might go and see her. 'Oh dear no,' exclaimed the Queen, 'There would only be what Brown calls Hell and hot water.'

Another time, when searching for an expression strong enough to describe the Belgian clergy, she settled on ' "Nasty Beggars", as Brown would say'.

Sometimes it was a bit of Brown's homespun philosophy she appreciated. His observation that 'it can't be very pleasant for a person themselves always to be cross' she thought 'so true and original.' Normally he himself was 'so cheerful'. When, however, he was in a brusque mood she happily put up with him, as when she arranged for a drive and he greeted her with 'What are ye daeing with that auld black dress on again? It's green-moulded'. (She went back in and changed it.) And he told her a number of times, probably quite rightly, that she 'didn't know her own mind for two minutes together'.

In the Highlands he was in his element. On foreign trips he was a liability. Not only was he ill-at-ease abroad, and consequently out of temper, but the fact that he wore the kilt in places where it had never been seen before was apt to draw crowds and destroy what little remained of the Queen's incognito. Nor, if one story is to be believed, did his down-to-earth manner always convey to foreigners what was intended. Victoria had arrived in Switzerland to find her bed had been lost in transit. Enterprising as ever, Brown set off in search of it and was quickly spotted by a tout from a local hotel.

'Can I help you, Monsieur?'

'Aye, ye can do that. I'm looking for a bed.'

'As I thought, Monsieur. Then permit me to suggest that you will find the best beds at the Hotel—.'

' 'Tis the Queen of England's bed I'm looking forre.'

'Ah, well, I am sorry. I can do nothing for Monsieur. The best bed we could find anywhere for you in this place is that of an Italian Princess—and she—well, she is turned eighty!'

Usually he was more successful in providing for Victoria's material comforts. When she thanked him for an unusually good cup of tea his reply was: 'Well, it should be, Ma'am, I put a grand nip o' whisky in it.' She did not normally care for tea on her outings. 'She don't much like tea,' he told an inquisitive Maid of

Honour, 'we tak oot biscuits and sperruts.' Equally frank was his answer to his Balmoral crony who remarked, 'Ye must see a lot o' grand folks in London, John.' 'Me and the Queen pays nae attention to them,' came the reply.

One of the 'grand folks' who was wise enough to pay attention to 'Mr. Brown' was Benjamin Disraeli, later the Earl of Beaconsfield. Anyone less like Brown than the wily Dizzy with his ingratiating ways it is difficult to imagine. Yet he too became Queen Victoria's 'dear friend'. She was forty-eight and he sixty-three when he, as he put it, 'climbed to the top of the greasy pole' and kissed hands as Prime Minister. But, as his account of the occasion shows, he was already a favourite. 'The Queen,' he revealed, 'came into the closet with a very radiant face, holding out her hand, and saying, "You must kiss hands," which I did immediately, very heartily, falling on my knee.' He followed up the ceremony with a letter: he had, he boldly proclaimed, 'nothing to offer but his devotion'. By the time he came to form his second ministry he was even more effusive. 'He knelt down,' the Queen recorded with obvious pleasure, 'and kissed hands, saying: "I plight my troth to the kindest of *Mistresses*!" '

What was the secret of the fantastic success with Queen Victoria of a man of Disraeli's unpromising background and chequered career? No doubt Henry Ponsonby was right when he said 'he has got the length of her foot exactly'. 'I think he must have spread his butter very thick,' suggested Augusta Stanley less kindly. Lord Clarendon was even more cynical: 'The Jew, who is "the most subtle beast in the field", has, like Eve's temptress, ingratiated himself with the Missus and made her forget that, in the opinion of the great and good, he has not one single element of a gentleman in his composition.' Queen Victoria was certainly no snob. She had nothing but admiration for the fact that the highest political office had gone to a man with Disraeli's disadvantages—coming from a race that was looked down on, born without great riches, his father (in her own words) 'a mere man of letters'. 'Mr. Disraeli,' she boasted, 'has achieved his present high position by his ability, his *wonderful, happy disposition* and the astounding way in which he carried through the Reform Bill, and I have nothing but praise for him.' Certainly he knew how to ingratiate himself, having particularly winning ways with the ladies. Princess Marie Louise reveals his approach:

> A young lady was taken to dinner one night by Gladstone and, the following night, by Disraeli. She was asked what impression these two celebrated men had made upon her. She replied thoughtfully: 'When I left the dining-room after sitting next to Mr. Gladstone I thought he was the cleverest man in England. But after sitting next to Mr. Disraeli I thought I was the cleverest woman in England!'

This goes a long way towards explaining how, irrespective of political views, Disraeli succeeded with the Queen while Gladstone was a ghastly failure. By his courtly attentions, by appearing to listen, by giving her the feeling that her opinions counted for something, Disraeli ended up as 'this great, wise and charming statesman, who is my very dear friend'. Gladstone, on the other hand, was a poor listener and ignored his wife's plea to make a fuss of the Queen. Hence, after an initial popularity, he went through an intermediate stage of 'I cannot find him very agreeable, as he talks so very much,' and ended up as 'the terrible old G man'.

Still, says G. E. Buckle in his mammoth study of Disraeli, it is absurd to suggest that the Queen's devotion to Disraeli was mainly due to flattery.

> This myth has sprung largely from Beaconfield's ingrained habit of attributing to himself, in his hatred of cant, lower motives than those from which he really acted. Two delightful sayings of his are quoted. He told Lord Esher that, in talking to the Queen, he observed a simple rule: 'I never deny; I never contradict; I sometimes forget.' And to Matthew Arnold, in a conversation shortly before his death, he said: 'You have heard me called a flatterer, and it is true. Everyone likes flattery, and when you come to royalty, you should lay it on with a trowel.'
> The Queen was too much inured to flattery to care for it . . . But she was a woman as well as a Queen, and Disraeli was her

only Minister since Melbourne who always bore the fact in mind. To women . . . his attitude throughout his life was one of chivalrous devotion. 'What wonder,' Lord Esher has well written, 'that his chivalrous devotion for the sex should have taken a deeper complexion when the personage was not merely a woman, but a Queen?'

For, in spite of his own disparaging remarks, Disraeli was as genuinely attached to the Queen as she was to him. Late in life he confessed 'I love the Queen—perhaps the only person in this world left to me that I do love.' This love manifested itself in strange ways. 'He is full of poetry, romance and chivalry,' was how Victoria summed up this side of him. It was a combination she found it difficult to resist. Even sending him some snowdrops could produce the most romantic reaction:

> . . . he thought that at first your Majesty had graciously bestowed upon him the stars of your Majesty's principal orders . . . Then in the middle of the night, it occurred to him that it might be all an enchantment, and that, perhaps, it was a Faery gift and came from another monarch: perhaps Queen Titania, gathering flowers, with her Court, in a soft sea-girt isle, and sending magic blossoms which, they say, turn the heads of those who receive them.

She sent him a valentine and received a reply calling her 'most gracious of beings'. Augusta Stanley might well write: 'She declares she has never had such letters in her life.' After she had helped him deal with one of his more difficult lieutenants he told her he 'perceived that a "Faery Queen" had waved her magic wand'. 'Faery' became his pet name for her.

In addition to his poetry and romance Disraeli, with his 'wonderful happy disposition', was most amusing company. As Buckle points out, he 'exhausted his resources of wit and humour, his stories of epigram and anecdote, for her Majesty's amusement'. Hence, like Lord Melbourne of old, he was a prized guest. Down at Windsor for dinner he would send the royal children into fits of laughter.

The Queen was in high spirits and wanted to know all dinner what Princess Christian and Prince Leopold were laughing at. As I never laugh at my own remarks my head was safe, and Her Majesty would scarcely decapitate her children. But I heard her say in German, smiling, 'What is he saying?'

She enjoyed his dry, self-deprecating sense of humour, as when he described himself as the blank page between the Old Testament and the New. 'Did he really say, "We authors, Ma'am"?' asks one of his biographers; 'the story has never been authenticated, but it deserves to be true'.

Transacting business in such circumstances was a pleasure for both of them. Having asked him to Balmoral for a week she begged him to stay a fortnight. When he kissed her hand in one audience, he confided to a friend, 'she actually gave me a squeeze'.

During an audience at Osborne his increasing infirmity even led to a significant loosening of Court etiquette:

> The Faery sent for me the instant I arrived. I can only describe my reception by telling you that I really thought she was going to embrace me. She was wreathed with smiles, and, as she talked, glided about the room like a bird . . . and then she said—'To think of your having gout all the time. How you must have suffered! And you ought not to stand now, you shall have a chair!'
>
> Only think of that! I remember that Lord Derby, after one of his illnesses, had an audience of Her Majesty, and he mentioned it to me as a proof of the Queen's favor, that Her Majesty had remarked to him how sorry she was she could not ask him to be seated, the etiquette was so severe.

The experience was later repeated: 'She says I am never to stand . . . When I took leave at the audience I would put my golden chair back in its place that a breach of etiquette should be kept secret. So I told her, and she smiled.'

Having once made the concession to Disraeli Victoria was to extend it to later Prime Ministers, though sitting with the aged and deaf Gladstone was no fun—he would draw up his chair as close as possible and put his ear to her face.

Analysing the strange friendship of Queen Victoria and Benjamin Disraeli, Lord Esher wrote:

> He was never in the least shy: he did not trouble to insinuate; he said what he meant in terms the most surprising, the most unconventional; and the Queen thought she had never in her life seen so amusing a person. He gratified her by his bold assumptions of her knowledge, she excused his florid adulation on the ground that it was 'Oriental', and she was pleased with the audacious ways in which he broke through the ice that surrounded her. He would ask, across the dinner-table, 'Madam, did Lord Melbourne ever tell Your Majesty you were not to do this or that?' and the Queen would take it as the best of jokes.

To sum up: she was amused, she was diverted, she gratified her old love of the *outré*, and she welcomed someone who was not in awe of her. Yet, in spite of everything, she still was not blind to Disraeli's peculiarities. 'He is very peculiar, but very clever and sensible and very conciliatory,' was her view when he first became Prime Minister. Ten years later, after reading one of his novels, she was still of the same opinion.

> Balmoral 31st October 1878—Finished reading *Coningsby*, a remarkable, strange book. I often recognise Lord Beaconsfield's language and feeling. There are some beautiful sentiments in it, and some very striking opinions, a sort of democratic conservatism, but the same large, patriotic views he holds now. The story is strange and the language too stilted and unnatural. Some of the characters are easily to be recognised. His love for, and faith in the Jews is very apparent.

If Disraeli laid on the flattery with a trowel the other facets of their relationship appealed to her more. As she said at the time of her Golden Jubilee, 'I don't want or like flattery, but I am very thankful and encouraged by these marks of affection and appreciation of my efforts'. Disraeli gave her affection and was lavish in expressing his appreciation. 'Gladstone treats her like a public department,' he once said, 'I treat her like a woman.' 'He understands me so well,' she admitted at the time of his death. In consequence, 'so long as he was there one felt, as with the old Duke of Wellington, a sense of security'.

But so long as he was there Disraeli insisted on maintaining his cynical pose. When asked on his death-bed whether he would like a visit from the Queen, his answer is said to have been completely in character: 'No, it is better not. She will only ask me to take a message to Albert.'

CHAPTER XII

Friendly Relations

Though subject to the same strains and stresses to be found in every family, Queen Victoria's relationship with her grown-up children was normally warm and affectionate. She could sometimes be difficult—but so could they. Why, asked Lady Churchill, when the Queen was suffering from a serious illness in 1871, had her children not been summoned? 'Good Heavens,' replied Sir Thomas Biddulph, who had been long enough at Court to know the score, 'that would have killed her at once.' Yet it was not every Victorian mama who could write to her daughter, as Queen Victoria did to the Princess Royal: 'My intercourse with you is so natural and open and I never feel any difficulty in pouring out my heart and mind to you.'

A relaxed relationship with the Prince of Wales took longer to develop. She could not help deploring his 'fast' way of life. She heartily agreed with the truth of Brown's remark that 'the only privacy the Prince of Wales wants is the privacy of the public highway'. 'The country and all of us,' she told him in her own downright fashion, 'would like to see you a little more *stationary*.' In spite of this she came increasingly to appreciate his good nature: he had, she found out, 'a loving and affectionate heart' and was 'so full of good and amiable qualities'. 'I am sure no Heir Apparent was ever so nice and unassuming as dear Bertie is.'

Her second son, Prince Alfred, was initially a bit of a trial. For one thing his private life left much to be desired. For another, his violin playing was excruciating to listen to. But there were compensations. Throwing grammar to the wind the Queen enthused to her eldest daughter: 'I think he gets liker and liker to blessed Papa!' The comparison could not be carried too far, though. When Alfred joined the navy a story went round London about how he managed to supplement his modest midshipman's allowance:

> . . . he soon discovered he could make a capital of his royal mother's letters. One day he came among the mids with a new letter, crying out, 'I'm sure you ought to give me £5 for this one—there's such a lot of good advice in it!'

Prince Arthur was easier to manage. Sir Howard McLintock, who was put in charge of him when he was fifteen, was impressed by the extent of the Queen's motherly interest in the boy, knitting him mittens and giving him a retriever dog. When he grew up her concern continued. 'Dear Arthur is looking very ill and alto-gether *not* well,' she declared on the eve of his marriage when he was approaching thirty. Her remedy was the simple old-fashioned one: 'He must be looked after and *dosed* for he is yellow and green.' As dear Arthur lived to the age of ninety-one his mother, as it happened, had no cause for alarm.

The youngest son, Prince Leopold, on the other hand, suffered from haemophilia and was never strong. Luckily he was both intelligent and high-spirited. When he became studious his mother joked about it to McLintock: 'The love of learning of little Prince Leo *not* inherited from her, she added with a laugh, she hated lessons, the Prince Consort on the contrary liked them above all else.' Leopold's French pronunciation, though, she thought abominable—'more like Chinese than anything else'. After his brothers had left home Leopold lived on with his mother, his relationship with her becoming a free and easy one. Eventually he married and, to his mother's surprise, fathered a family. His first child—Princess Alice, later Countess of Athlone—was born at a time when the Queen had sprained a leg. So she hobbled down the corridors to congratulate the happy couple, only to be over-come by her sense of the ridiculous. 'He was lying on one sofa, she on another and when I came as a third helpless creature, it had quite a ludicrous effect.'

Death had a habit of striking unexpectedly at Queen Victoria—three of her children, including Leopold, died before she did—but as she grew older she seemed better able to bear her losses. Old anniversaries and Court mourning were kept up, but somehow without the former depression. When the Czar of Russia died the band at Balmoral was at first stopped from playing in the evenings. Soon however the Queen allowed herself to be persuaded that it was possible to 'mourn to music' and playing was resumed. The Prince Consort's birthday was regarded as an occasion for rejoicing—and for giving extraordinary presents. One year, for example, according to the Queen's Journal, 'When I came down to breakfast I gave Beatrice a mounted enamel photograph of our dear Mausoleum, and a silver belt of Montengrin workmanship. After breakfast I gave my faithful Brown an oxidised silver biscuit-box, and some onyx studs. He was greatly pleased with the former, and the tears came to his eyes, and he said "It is too much." '

Queen Victoria had a penchant for unusual gifts. 'I send you,' she wrote on her eldest daughter's thirtieth birthday, 'the copy of a picture painted of dear Beatrice last year, a warm Scotch cloak with the Prussian colours and a new biscuit box of Aberdeenshire granite.' Biscuit boxes were obviously highly-prized objects in royal circles in those days—perhaps Queen Victoria would have done well to have given one to her cousin Mary Adelaide who at one stage was reduced to keeping her biscuits in a hat box. Once she sent her grandson, the future Wilhelm II, a silver statuette of the Prince Consort conquering sin. It did not have the effect intended.

One important reason for the ageing Queen Victoria's renewed interest in life was the presence round her of young grandchildren. As of old, she loved happy smiling young faces: 'Dear little things, I like to see them so much at home with me.' No doubt the naturalness of children accounted for a good deal of their appeal. At a time when adults were treating her with more and more reverence childish high spirits must have seemed like a breath of fresh air. Even if she could no longer romp she could unbend with them. One grandson had vivid memories of her sense of fun—'and her wonderful laugh!' 'I well remember driving with her many times when I was a boy. We would make jokes and return to the Castle aching with laughter.' The future Kaiser and his brothers could be a bit of a handful, though. Young Waldemar once shocked his grandmama by letting loose his pet crocodile at her feet. Another time her sense of propriety was outraged, the culprit being variously described as the future Wilhelm II and the future George V:

... His grandmother had occasion to reprove him for want of manners at table one day. As a punishment he was sent under the table when sweets were being served. After an interval pardon was asked and granted, and the culprit ordered to come out. This he did—but in the same condition Nature made him. The Queen was very angry at the time, but has often related and laughed at the joke.

As the children of the Prince of Wales tended to be over-indulged by their parents visits to their grandmother had less appeal for them. These children were a disappointment in other ways. The eldest, Albert Victor, was a seven-months child. 'That poor bit of a thing wrapped in cotton' was the Queen's description of her first sight of him. She was prone to describe him as 'a fairy': 'Little Albert Victor is a great darling but a fairy.' Nor were the babies that followed any better in her eyes: 'They are such miserable, puny little children (each weaker than the preceding one).' Princess Helena's daughter, Marie Louise, was another early victim of the Queen's overriding sense of honesty:

My mother was rather delicate and, under doctor's orders, spent a winter in the south of France. We children were then 'parked' with our grandmother. I was not quite two years old, and this is the telegram that she sent to my parents: 'Children very well, but poor little Louise very ugly' ... Later on, when I heard of this disastrous description, I reproached Grandmama and said: 'Grandmama, how could you have sent such an unkind telegram?'
She replied: 'My dear child, it was only the truth!'

Apart from her family Queen Victoria came mainly into contact with her Official. Household and her personal servants. In choosing those who were to serve her she went for people who were straight. She preferred them to be amusing and above all she liked those who had spirit. Randall Davidson, when Dean of Windsor, had direct experience of the Queen's reaction to someone who stood up to her. After John Brown's death he took it upon himself to express disapproval of her intention to publish what would have been a highly embarrassing book about John Brown. He then offered to resign. A week or two of total silence followed. Finally, 'she sent for me on some other matter of a totally different nature, and was more friendly than ever, and we have never heard another word about the proposed book'. 'My belief,' he concluded, 'is that she liked and trusted best those who occasionally incurred her wrath provided she had reason to think their motives good.' She certainly adored her jolly, handsome son-in-law, Henry of Battenberg and he, said the Empress Eugénie, was 'not in the least awed by the Queen ... he gives his opinion frankly whenever he finds an opportunity'. Mary Bulteel, the Maid of Honour who married Henry Ponsonby, was popular for similar reasons: 'The Queen was deeply interested in anyone who cared for acting and music; and when these tastes were combined with an absolute fearless character it appealed to her imagination.' One remark of Mary's shows how much she and the Queen were on the same wavelength—'Towards the end of dinner Colonel Wilde and Uncle Charles tried to speak *sotto voce* to one another—I said low to Stockmar, "That will never do, they are both as deaf as posts." "Yes!" the Queen said across, "both!"'

Sir Henry Ponsonby did not retain his post as Private Secretary for twenty-five years because he was a yes-man. Typical of his attitude was the advice he gave the future George V whom the Queen asked to assume the name of Albert: 'He would gladly lay down his life for the Queen, but if she asked him to call himself Thomas he would certainly refuse.' What Ponsonby, like Disraeli, did show was tact and appreciation of the fact that the Queen was a woman:

When she insists that two and two make five I say that I cannot help thinking they make four. She replies that there may be some truth in what I say, but she knows they make five. I drop the discussion. But X goes on with it, bringing proofs, arguments and sayings of her own. The Queen can't abide it.

Ponsonby's tactics were well-conceived, as he demonstrated when the Empress of Russia died and there was discussion over who would represent the Queen at the funeral. Ponsonby suggested the Duke of Edinburgh.

The Queen said 'No of course he couldn't.' I said 'Of course he couldn't.' But as I did not know why, I got back to him in the course of conversation and said it was a pity he couldn't. So she telegraphed to ask him if he could and he said he would.

This type of approach also made for pleasant working conditions. 'The Queen and I,' Ponsonby once told his wife, 'at the present moment live rather in a mutual admiration society for she writes a letter saying the Duke of Cumberland is a fool and I say it is perfect, and then I write a letter saying he is a damned fool and she says it is admirable.' His secret was not to take her too seriously. He was not above transmitting her remarks in the manner of John Brown. 'Princess B. seemed to think it possible H.M. would go to one Drawing Room,' runs one of his reports, 'but H.M. in sad and mournful tones said she would be damned if she would.'

It was one of Queen Victoria's odder habits to transmit her requests in writing or through an intermediary. Ponsonby, for example, one day received a message through Lady Ely, to the effect that his trousers were too long. He reacted in characteristic fashion. 'Of course I pinned them up and of course the Maids of Honour roared at our serious discussion upon the length of trousers and of course I chalked the proper length on Robertson's trousers. Whereat there was much chaff and Jane Ely said she was sorry I took it in that light as it was only a very gentle hint and not meant to offend—which it certainly did not.' His predecessor, General Grey, had not always been so co-operative. In Grey's day, it was recalled, 'a young lady-in-waiting appeared (for some days) rather heavily made up. "Dear General Grey," said the Queen, "will tell her". When the message was conveyed to him he was heard to murmur: "Dear General Grey will do nothing of the kind."'

Another peculiarity which grew with the years was the Queen's dislike of members of her Household marrying. The men she imagined would discuss her private life with their wives, as of course they did. The ladies who married in her service normally gave up their posts. In her widowhood she was, as she said, 'very dependent on those I am accustomed to', and came to dread parting with old friends. Such a reaction is understandable in someone who spent her life trying to surround herself with a feeling of security. Hence she deeply regretted that Lady Augusta Bruce, on whom in her early widowhood she had come to depend, 'at forty-one most unnecessarily decided to marry!!' As the years advanced breaks of this kind were felt more keenly than ever. As Victoria told the wife of a retiring Ambassador, 'at her age she rather dreaded saying goodbye, also seeing new faces, and she was very sorry we were going'. Maids of Honour, such as Marie Adeane, leaving Court to get married, found their final audience, full of tearful kisses, most painful.

The Queen's attitude to servants was, to say the least, unusual. As she herself affirmed, it was one more trait that could be traced back to her childhood: 'I was taught from the first to beg my maid's pardon for any naughtiness or rudeness towards her; a feeling I have ever retained, and think everyone should own their fault in a kind of way to any one, be he or she the lowest—if one has been rude or injured them by word or deed, especially those below you.'

From her early years too she had been apt to shed floods of tears on hearing of the death of an old servant. When she came to the throne one of her first acts was to settle pensions on those who had previously served her, right down to the crossing-sweeper outside Kensington Palace. Her own children were brought up as she had been. The Princess Royal, for one, was frequently admonished for not showing a proper respect for servants. Prince Arthur told Hector Bolitho that, when as a boy he arrived at Balmoral, '"before anything else" he was sent by the Queen to shake hands with the servants'. All his life King Edward VII made a point of saying 'thank you' to them, and grandchildren were expected to show the same consideration.

Weaknesses among servants the Queen was quite prepared to tolerate. 'Her idea was that when people were well-bred and well-educated, they should know better than to make mistakes,' one of her grandsons explained, 'but she would forgive humble people, whatever they did.' Thus excessive drinking by servants, in England as well as in Scotland, was something to be accepted. The Princess Royal once received the following matter-of-fact account from her mother:

> You remember poor King who used to be the nursery servant— and then Papa's gardrobier etc.—and had to be put lower and lower for drinking? He died this morning of delirium tremens! Papa appointed Archie McDonald his Gardrobier—Bray getting another place; he also tipples.

A footman, well-known for drunkenness, once in a stupor nearly caused a fire at Windsor Castle. The Master of the Household thought that this at last provided the opportunity to get rid of him. He therefore had a full report on the man's drunkenness sent to the Queen. She read the account but all she did was write two words in the margin:

> 'Poor man.'

CHAPTER XIII

Moving with the Times

As the years went by and the Queen adjusted to her widowed state the self-denying resolutions she had made when Albert died were gradually laid aside. Within a few years singing was heard in her drawing-room again. Prima donna Christine Nilsson came to Windsor and was enchanted at the way in which her enthusiastic hostess kept asking for more. The Queen's own fine singing voice was heard again at the beginning of 1867 when she accompanied Princess Louise on the piano, 'even trying a little myself'. Some years later she surprised her ladies by selecting for herself the music from *H.M.S. Pinafore* and proceeding to sing:

'For I'm called little Buttercup—dear Little Buttercup,
'Though I could never tell why,
'But still I'm called Buttercup, poor Little Buttercup,
'Sweet Little Buttercup I!'

Even dancing made its return to her drawing room. When nearly sixty she proudly noted: 'The Marine Band played during dinner, and afterwards the ladies and gentlemen all joined us, and we had a little impromptu dance in the Drawing-room'. It was quite like old times: 'We had five dances and I danced a Quadrille, and a valse (which I had not done for eighteen years) with dear Arthur, who valses extremely well, and I found I could do it as well as ever!'

In time she regained her ability to enjoy quite new experiences. The seemingly miraculous invention of the telephone intrigued her. 'After dinner we went to the Council Room and saw the telephone. A Professor Bell explained the whole process, which is most extraordinary . . . But it is rather faint, and one must hold the tube close to one's ear.' Just as she had made full use of the telegraph system, so she later had the telephone installed; and the Princess of Wales, staying at Abergeldie, complained that the line from Balmoral never stopped ringing.

Indeed any suggestion that Queen Victoria as she got older was against all new inventions is quite false. When her grandson the Kaiser was coming to Osborne she had the dining room fitted up with another miracle of the age, electric light. With all the pride of a young bride she declared that 'the room was beautiful with the electric lights and the beautiful ornaments, and was much admired'. In this field she was merely carrying on in the tradition of Albert's day when the new gaslighting had been installed in Buckingham Palace. She and Albert had also been keen photographers from very early days. Again Victoria retained her enthusiasm into her old age. In the 1890s she took part in some of the earliest 'moving pictures'. 'We were all photographed by Downey by the new cinematograph process, which makes moving pictures by winding off a reel of film,' she wrote at Balmoral. Two months later she attended what must have been the first royal film performance, 'where so-called "animated pictures" were shown off'. She was most impressed: 'It is a very wonderful process, representing people, their movements and actions as if they were alive.' The gramophone was another invention she tested out. She recorded her voice on one of the earliest discs in order to convey a greeting to the Emperor Menelek of Ethiopia. He was duly appreciative, stood to attention while listening to it, and had an artillery salute fired in its honour.

One discovery on which Victoria had most decided views was chloroform. What these views were her granddaughter Marie, the later Queen of Rumania, discovered unexpectedly as a young woman when she went on a drive with her grandmother. At first both of them felt rather shy.

Gradually our mutual reserve began to melt and I found myself answering her questions with animation; besides she had a sweet way of laughing at unexpected moments, a silvery, really amused little laugh, and this laugh bridged some of the distance between us. She asked me about the country I had gone to, about the climate, the people, their habits, their politics . . . She asked, of course, about my husband . . . she was even interested in the servants . . . And then turning towards me she suddenly sprang this question upon me: 'Did they give you chloroform when your children were born?'

Oh, dear, why did she ask me this? Was she one of those people who disapproved of a woman's hour of travail being eased, thanks to the inventions of modern science? . . . In quite a small voice I therefore confessed that though I had not actually been put to sleep, towards the end the edge of my suffering had been taken from me by that blessed anaesthetic.

And now for the scolding, for the sermon, for the expression of a royal lady's scorn; for Queen Victoria, no doubt, was a spartan and would wholeheartedly despise me for my cowardliness. But what was my astonishment when I heard a sweet, crystalline peal of laughter, and Grandmama, with that almost apologetic shrug of her shoulders, declared: 'Quite right, my dear, I was only given chloroform with my ninth and last baby. [It was actually with her eighth.] It had, alas! not been discovered before, and I assure you, my child, I deeply deplore the fact that I had to bring eight children into the world without its precious aid.'

In no field of human activity was there a greater change during Queen Victoria's lifetime than in transportation. She was a girl when George Stephenson was making his trials with the railway locomotive. She lived to see railways spread throughout the world. She saw ships change from wood and sail to iron and steam. Her later life saw the advent of the motor car. By the time of her death the Wright brothers were already engaged on their flying experiments at Kitty Hawk.

She did not see her first railway train till the year of her accession. 'We went to see the Railroad near Hersham, and saw the steam carriage pass with surprising quickness, striking sparks as it flew along the railroad, enveloped in clouds of smoke and making a loud noise. It is a curious thing indeed.' 'Steam carriages are very dangerous,' she decided and it was not till she was twenty three that she ventured on one. Her first journey, from Slough to Paddington, was complicated by the fact that the Master of the Horse, to preserve his prerogatives, insisted that he should direct the train. Eventually a compromise was worked out and she was able to enjoy her trip. It was, she discovered, 'free from dust and crowds and heat' and altogether 'I am quite charmed by it'. As the royal taste for distant holidays developed Victoria became a seasoned railway traveller. She was among the first to have had sleeping accommodation provided on a train, albeit of a somewhat primitive kind. 'We drove to Euston Square Station, whence we started at nine p.m.,' she wrote triumphantly from Edinburgh in 1859; 'Matresses were arranged on the floor and we came down quite comfortably arriving at eight this morning.'

She also prided herself on her love of the sea and ships. 'No help, I thank you, I am used to this,' she had boasted as a young Queen descending a ship's ladder. When nearly sixty she took herself off to visit H.M.S. *Thunderer,* and was delighted by her own continued agility: 'I found the ladders rather steep, but I have not forgotten my *sea legs.*' But the primitive motor car, when it appeared towards the end of her reign, she could not stomach at all. The Master of the Horse took note of her feelings:

> When motors were first introduced Queen Victoria saw a picture of the Prince of Wales in an open motor, wearing a high hat which had been shaken or blown on to his nose. Her Majesty said to me, 'I hope you will never allow one of those horrible machines to be used in my stables. I am told they smell exceedingly nasty, and are very shaky and disagreeable conveyances altogether'. So long as H.M. lived there never was any motor in the royal use.

And it has to be confessed that, at this stage of automobile development, there was a good deal in what she said.

She also disliked the exceedingly nasty smell of tobacco. Again her views have to be looked at in the light of the situation at the time. In her youth smoking was not accepted in polite society even among men. Even the normally tolerant Melbourne had fiercely denounced the habit—'I always make a great row about it; if I smell tobacco I swear perhaps for half an hour.' Therefore Queen Victoria came to regard the smoking of tobacco at Court rather as Queen Elizabeth II might be expected to regard the smoking of pot. Even in her later years, though the tobacco habit spread, standards of behaviour in public did not change much. One of the German Ambassadors pointed out:

> . . . in the late Victorian age it was positively rude to smoke in the company of ladies, and unpardonable to smell of tobacco . . . No smoking at all was allowed in the royal palaces, not even in the guests bedrooms. I remember, on a visit to Windsor, seeing Count Hatzfeldt, who could not live without a cigarette, lying in his pyjamas on his bedroom floor, blowing the smoke up the chimney.

By this stage in fact there were certain facilities for palace smoking. Though the Queen still disapproved of tobacco, the younger members of her family, in Fritz Ponsonby's words, 'smoked like chimneys'. One of the stories current in mid-Victorian society suggested that, even when smoking in the royal residences was totally forbidden, the Queen's sons appropriated a room at Windsor for the purpose. Panic ensued when they learnt that their mother intended to make an inspection of every room in the Castle. Luckily the Prince of Wales thought up a sure way out of the dilemma: 'Write W.C. up over the door.' The first official victory for the smoking lobby came in the late 1860s when the newly-married Princess Helena arrived at Balmoral with her husband, Prince Christian.

> The Queen heard to her horror that he smoked. It was not so bad as if he drank, but still it was a distinct blemish on his other-wise impeccable character. The Queen, however, decided to be broadminded and actually to give him a room where he could

indulge his habit. A small room was found near the servants' quarters which could only be reached by crossing the open kitchen courtyard, and in this bare room was placed a wooden chair and a table. She looked upon this room as a sort of opium den.

When Prince Henry married Princess Beatrice in the 1880s and came to live with his mother-in-law he exercised that male charm to which the Queen was always susceptible. As a result the regime was liberalised. A more comfortable room was provided at Balmoral and smoking allowed in the billiard room at Osborne.

This still did not provide an official outlet for the ladies. One of the Queen's granddaughters, the later Marchioness of Milford Haven, was to recall 'secretly smoking up chimneys and out of windows'. Once, she remembered, 'one of the young maids of honour, Amy Lambart, who, though a smoker herself, had come without any cigarettes and whose room was below ours, was supplied by me with a few at a time let down by a piece of string from window to window'. In spite of these precautions the Queen knew that her granddaughters smoked. Out of doors at Balmoral Lady Milford Haven found her grandmother surprisingly open-minded on the subject. 'Guessing that I probably had cigarettes about me, and the midges being especially annoying, she bade me smoke to keep them away, and even took one of my cigarettes, giving a few puffs at it.' (Not that she liked it—'She declared she thought the taste horrible.') At other times she actually pandered to people's taste for tobacco. When she found out that John Brown's aunt liked to smoke she made a point of giving her tobacco; and during the Egyptian campaign of the early 1880s she even wrote to the Secretary for War offering to supply it to the troops.

For most inhabitants of the royal residences the icy temperatures were a far worse trial than the smoking restrictions. Due probably to slightly raised blood pressure Queen Victoria did not feel the cold. Even in her youth she abominated heat. 'The Queen,' runs her account of a drive when she was twenty, 'thought that the air

was like as if it came out of an oven.' In old age she wrote with
equal vividness: 'The heat was quite terrific and I felt dissolved.'
She was convinced that it was unhealthy. Henry Ponsonby over-
heard 'a fierce discussion' over whether it would be better to be
marooned at the Equator or the North Pole. 'Princess Beatrice was
for the Equator but the Queen fierce for the North Pole.' Once,
when she was seventy-seven, she apologised for enjoying cold
weather so much—'I always feel so brisk.'

In hot weather the Empress Eugénie noticed that the royal
dinner table was decorated with blocks of ice surrounded by
begonias. Entering the Queen's railway carriage on a fine day
Marie Mallet 'nearly plunged headlong into a huge footbath full
of ice'. In winter, while others froze, the Queen felt comfortable.
Lord Redesdale arrived at Balmoral late one year to find that,
though it was 'bitterly cold and snowing', there was no sign of
the Queen or her entourage. A note from Sir Henry Ponsonby
explained their absence: 'We are off on a picnic.' As the Empress
Eugénie told her attendants, when she was having tea on her
drives with the Queen 'she not infrequently saw flakes of snow
falling into her cup'. 'The wind was so cold,' wrote a Maid of
Honour after a twenty-four mile drive with her mistress, 'my
face turned first blue and then crimson and by dinner time I looked
as if I had been drinking hard for a week.'

Yet if the physical discomforts of other human beings sometimes escaped her, Queen Victoria was quickly aroused by the
discomfort of animals. Vivisection, she announced, caused 'her
whole nature to boil over'. Ministers were apt to receive long
memoranda on what she called her 'poor dear friends the dogs'.
Her regard for horses was so well known that when her carriage
came to a steep hill her gillie felt obliged to get off the box to ease
the load. Unfortunately it had very little effect, the gillie was so
fat and distressed by his efforts that the occupants of the next
carriage frequently felt it necessary to give him a lift. It was because
of the horses that she disliked polo. 'The Queen wishes Prince
Arthur would not encourage Polo,' she pleaded with his governor,
'it is really cruel.'

In one respect, perhaps, Queen Victoria was ahead of her time. She was a most decided advocate for the use of the water-closet. When the Princess Royal settled in Germany her mother felt it necessary to send her what she described as 'a long story about a very horrid subject'. As the subject of the story was so horrid the poor Queen was hard put to it to find enough euphemisms to convey her meaning. She began by referring to the 'very necessary conveniences, which are totally wanting in Germany and really it makes one's life very uncomfortable and very unwholesome'. 'Now,' she continued, 'I told you last year that my aunt the Langravine sent for a person from here to make a number of these really necessary affairs . . . For you I think such a person might be very useful in engineering one or two at least of these affairs . . . I am sure you would be benefiting all Germany if they could be generally introduced.'

She herself practised what she preached. When about to pay a visit to Coburg she remembered the lack of these 'affairs' and arranged for a 'person' to 'engineer' one for her own use. Her granddaughter, Princess Alice, shows that in instructing the works superintendant the Queen left nothing to chance: 'She concluded her lengthy and detailed instructions with a final admonition "and mind you test it and sit on it and make sure it is the right height."'

The finished affair is still one of the sights of Coburg.

CHAPTER XIV

Not so Victorian

In spite of a reputation to the contrary Queen Victoria never became the narrow-minded Victorian so despised in the the twentieth century. The views she formulated before the Victorian Age got under way remained unchanged till the day she died. She never, for example, made a fetish out of church-going. During their marriage she and Albert did not see the necessity of going to church every Sunday; and when the Queen was seventy one of her granddaughters was still reporting 'We did not go to 'kirk' to-day —Grandmama did not feel inclined'. Her main concession to sabbatarianism was a characteristic one: the servants should not be made to work more than was necessary. Hence her condition when Princess Helena Victoria asked whether she and the Maids of Honour might play tennis on a Sunday: 'Grandmama's reply was, "Yes, so long as you pick up the balls yourself. Being Sunday, I do not think it right to make others work for your amusement."'

Not everyone in late Victorian times appreciated the breadth of her views. Arthur Balfour for one, as Fritz Ponsonby recalls, got himself involved in unnecessary subterfuge by telling her he was going for a Sunday afternoon walk when really he had arranged to play golf with the Duke of York. Later when she asked the Duke the same question he told her the truth, merely adding that he was sure she would not mind as they would carry their own clubs. 'This downright answer was clearly the right one,' says Fritz Ponsonby, 'but of course it put Arthur Balfour in a difficult position, and the Queen was much amused at catching him out, as she expressed it, "telling a fib".'

Nor were Victoria's views on gambling as cut-and-dried as might be supposed. Though she objected to excessive gambling for high stakes among the 'fast set', she herself enjoyed the occasional mild flutter. One year at Derby time when she was turned sixty Henry Ponsonby was amused to find she had 'taken up a sporting line'. 'She talks of Lord Hartington's horse and the Duke of Westminster's horse as if she were on Epsom Downs.' She even got up a lottery and took two tickets herself. (But her luck was out—Henry Ponsonby drew the winner, Ben d'Or.) Usually, though, her gambling instinct in later life centred round much more homely objects such as lotteries organised for her grandchildren for the fairy on top of the Christmas tree.

On religion the Queen held strong views but not always conventional ones. She had a particular dislike of what she called 'cold books on religion' and hated long boring sermons. Here at least she was following in her father's footsteps. 'I like your sermons very much,' the Duke of Kent is said to have told the Dean of Chester. When the Dean bowed the Duke went on '—because they are so short.' She had no love for fire and brimstone. After Dr. MacGregor, in her presence at Crathie, preached a sermon on the devil he asked Princess Louise whether her mother had enjoyed it. 'She said,' Henry Ponsonby reported, 'she had not heard but that she should think not, as the Queen did not altogether believe in the devil. MacGregor looked with a pitying eye and only said "puir body".' He would have been even more shocked had he known how much superstition this august parishioner had picked up in the Highlands: 'In Scotland nobody would marry in May as it is "so unlucky,"' she eagerly told her eldest daughter. Quoting a number of unfortunate May marriages she concluded, 'I never let one of our family marry in that month'. Once she sent a sick son-in-law a message which ran 'Thank God and touch wood you are so much better'—a case of trying to have the best of both worlds.

One 'Victorian' attribute which Queen Victoria did have in full measure was a sense of feminine modesty. How shocked she would have been had she known that her great contemporary, the Dowager Empress of China, used to clap her hands at garden parties and ask her ladies whether any of them wanted to spend a penny. For as Victoria once admitted, 'the animal side of our nature is to me—too dreadful'. In her youth she had confessed to Melbourne that 'anatomical descriptions' were to her 'very dis-agreeable', and when nearly forty was still begging the Princess Royal, then expecting her first baby, 'never to lose the modesty of a young girl towards others (without being prude)'. 'I myself,' she explained, 'remained particular to a degree (indeed feel so now) and often feel shocked by the confidences of other married ladies.' She was staggered by the lack of inhibition shown by her fat, un-married cousin Mary: 'Fancy . . . her asking *Papa*—if you were very sick ! ! ! a thing I should not ask hardly any gentleman ! ! and then very doubtful talk about wet nurses.'

To Victoria the whole process of human reproduction was distasteful. 'I positively think those ladies who are always enceinte quite disgusting; it is more like a rabbit or guinea pig than any-thing else and really it is not very nice.' 'There is Lady Kildare who has two a year one in January and one in December—and always is so whenever one sees her ! Now there are no end of jokes about her.' The Queen conveniently forgot that when she herself was newly married she had her first two children within a year of one another. 'One's feelings of propriety God knows receive a shock enough in marriage alone.' Her attitude to sex was summed up in her lament 'We poor creatures are born for Man's pleasure and amusement'.

When her own daughters started having families she became quite upset. 'Our children have (alas!) such swarms of children,' she complained, overlooking the fact that not one of them had as many children as she had had. The sight of the Princess of Wales's new-born daughter—'a little red lump was all I saw'—gave the honest grandmother further food for thought: '. . . I fear the seventh grand-daughter and fourteenth grandchild becomes a very uninteresting thing—for it seems to me to go on like the rabbits in Windsor Park !' When the Princess Royal talked of 'giving life to an immortal soul' she made it clear that she did not share her feelings. 'I think much more of being a cow or dog in such moments when our poor nature becomes very animal and unecstatic.' The Princess accordingly accused her mother of not liking babies. 'You know perfectly well,' came the downright reply, 'that I do not hate babies (quite the contrary if they are pretty) but I do hate the inordinate worship of them and the more disgusting details of their animal existence, which I try to ignore.'

These last words were significant for, at heart, on such matters Queen Victoria was an escapist. 'I can't read these books with descriptions of immorality,' she once admitted, 'I have enough that is painful and distressing to go through in reality.' She blamed the 'fashionables' among the upper classes, who got into the divorce courts, for setting such a bad example, and for lacking what she called 'delicacy of feeling'. 'Modern manners' in the Gay Nineties, according to Bernard Mallet, 'horrified' her.

She had heard dreadful stories of modern children, of parents like Lady Lytton allowing her girls to visit without her, horrified to hear no-one now learnt quadrilles, to hear of 'kitchen lancers' and Washington Posts! But modern manners not so modern perhaps. Her story of the young Crimean Officer whose letter to his mother was sent to H.M. to read: it began 'I have told all the fellows what a jolly old female you are'; Female! The Queen had no desire to read more!

Her attitude to engaged couples did adjust somewhat to the mood of the times. Back in the 1850s she had taken it as her duty constantly to chaperone the Princess Royal and her fiancé. It had proved to be a great bore. Fritz, it transpired, was fond of kissing and this created problems. Now neither the Queen nor Albert was against kissing *per se*. During their own engagement, when he had the opportunity, he had 'clasped me tenderly in his arms and kissed me again and again'. Hence, when Vicky and Fritz first became engaged the Queen was delighted when Vicky 'threw herself into his arms, and kissed him with a warmth which was responded to by Fritz again and again and I would not for the world have missed so touching and beautiful a sight'. But during the long engagement that followed constant kissing did not seem quite proper so life for the chaperone had been very trying.

Luckily by the time it came to the engagement of her youngest daughter things were easier. There was, as she told Vicky with evident relief, 'no kissing etc. (which Beatrice dislikes) which used to try me so with dear Fritz'. Still, as Prince Louis of Battenberg found out when he became engaged to one of the Queen's grand-daughters, there were still difficulties: 'I was only allowed to see my fiancée by stealth, as the Queen did not approve of engaged couples "spooning".' She really did not think it right, either, for them to go walking or driving on their own—'very American' in her opinion. Nevertheless, after she had seen the otherwise exemplary Prince Arthur out driving with his fiancée, she began to turn a blind eye. By the time the future Czar Nicholas II became engaged to another of her granddaughters things had relaxed so much that he was surprised at the old lady's easy-going attitude. 'Granny has been very friendly and even allowed us *to go out for drives* without a chaperone,' he told his mother, 'I confess I didn't expect that!'

It is a grave mistake to regard Queen Victoria as sanctimonious. True, in her capacity as Queen she recognised the importance, in-deed the necessity, of setting a good example. She was therefore, as Arthur Ponsonby expressed it, 'obedient to conventions be-cause they conveyed to her a standard which it might be dangerous to disregard'. This did not necessarily mean that she personally agreed with all these conventions. As the daughter of Lord Salisbury, her last Prime Minister, emphasised: 'The rigid ex-clusion from her Court which she meted out to open offenders in this connection was a function of her office, not an outcome of her impulses. She held herself to be the guardian of social purity . . . Lord Salisbury always strenuously denied that she had any trace of either Pharisaism or Puritanism.'

When she came to the throne she accepted the conventions then prevailing with regard to excluding certain categories of people from being received at Court. She insisted, however, on proof of wrongdoing before any exclusion was imposed. In later years it pleased her to relax the regulations somewhat. 'Lady Blandford came by,' she wrote after a reception in 1887, 'I having allowed poor divorced ladies, who have had to divorce their husbands owing to cruelty, or misbehaviour, but are in no way to blame themselves, to appear at Court.' Convinced of the justice of this step she then suggested to Lord Salisbury that foreign divorcees should be received on the same basis. Only when he pointed out 'the risk of admitting American women of light character' did she agree that it might be best to leave well alone.

Her private opinions on moral misdemeanours were in fact exceedingly charitable. Queen Isabella of Spain, for example, having been married to a man who was impotent, lived a life of such immorality that all Europe was scandalised. To Queen Victoria, however, she was 'a most unfortunate woman'. When she became pregnant Victoria pronounced it 'a very good thing'. 'No one,' she ventured to suggest, 'will cavil who the real *father* is considering her very peculiar and distressing marriage—for *she* poor young creature is in no wise to blame.' Further down the social ladder excuses for unorthodox moral behaviour were again forthcoming. One of the Princess Royal's ladies in Berlin caused a sensation by running off with a man without afterwards marrying him. She was condemned by society generally but not by Queen Victoria, who thought the ménage '½ crazy but holy'.

A cold heartless world—or a very severe or religious one— will not understand—but God will! To me there is such a vast difference between heartless wicked immorality, like one sees, alas! constantly—especially in the higher classes, and one noble passion when all the feelings and aspirations are pure and noble— and when only, perhaps from the impossibility of money, or rank, or God knows what, the outward earthly form cannot be given by men!

There was further disagreement with German opinion over a cousin of the future Queen Mary. The girl had been seduced by a footman and, when it was discovered that she was pregnant, was disowned by her family. Queen Victoria was shocked not by the girl but by the family's behaviour. It was, she most emphatically declared, 'too awful and shameful and almost sinful' to have sent the girl away. 'I hear from a reliable source that the *family* have forbidden the poor unhappy girl's name being mentioned in the family. . . . I think it is too wicked.'

Such tolerance and broadmindedness extended into other un-expected fields. If the Queen heard a broad joke, for instance, she was apt to become convulsed with laughter. Stories which revealed men in an embarrassing position appear to have had a strong appeal. Says Hector Bolitho:

> One night at dinner, somebody was talking about the Zulu war and they said the Zulus came over the top of the hill 'like a swarm of cockroaches'. A man at the table in the zest of his spontaneous wit corrected the speaker and offered another simile in the place of cockroaches, frankly phallic and very funny. The company became rigid. After a moment the Queen laughed—alone.

Another time she roared with laughter when telling Henry Ponsonby how shocked Sir Thomas Biddulph had been by the suggested design for a campaign medal—'Roman soldiers with nothing—nothing at all—but helmets on!' The future Kaiser also had a story to tell of his grandmother in this earthy mood. It involved old Admiral Foley whom she invited to luncheon to report on the tragic sinking of the *Eurydice*.

> After she had exhausted this melancholy subject, my grand-mother, in order to give the conversation a more cheerful turn, inquired after his sister, whom she knew well, whereon the Admiral, who was hard of hearing and still pursuing his train of thought about the *Eurydice*, replied in his stentorian voice: 'Well, Ma'am, I am going to have her turned over and take a good look at her bottom and have it well scraped.'
>
>   The effect of this answer was stupendous. My grandmother put down her knife and fork, hid her face in her handkerchief and shook and heaved with laughter till the tears rolled down her face.

Considering this side of the Queen it was in some ways a misfortune for her that as she advanced into old age she became a legend in her own lifetime. Even though she remained at heart a simple, homely soul—still, as in Creevey's day, 'dying to be more so'—she came increasingly to inspire awe. As a middle-aged widow, anxious for peace and quiet, she attracted to herself profound respect and devotion. With the passing of the years there was added to this a new ingredient: the reverence she was accorded as she became an apparently-permanent institution. The jitters this produced have helped build up her reputation as a frightening matriarch which has been handed down to us as the real Queen Victoria.

The awe-struck attitudes of those about her took many years to perfect. Henry Ponsonby witnessed an early indication of the trends at Sandringham in 1871.

> Yesterday Haig and I went out towards the garden by a side door when we were suddenly nearly carried away by a stampede of royalties, headed by the Duke of Cambridge and brought up by Leopold, going as fast as they could. We thought it was a mad bull. But they cried out: 'The Queen, the Queen,' and we all dashed into the house again and waited behind the door till the road was clear. When Haig and I were alone we laughed immensely.

Ponsonby may have laughed but his own family was guilty of getting into just such a panic. 'The Queen hated fires,' noted one of his sons. 'Warned one day at Osborne that the Queen was coming to pay a visit, the Ponsonby family set to work to remove the drawing-room fire in a bucket of water, quickly opening all the windows to get rid of the stench.'

Just as the Queen was known to hate hot rooms, so her dislike of meeting anyone she knew when out for her afternoon drive was well-known. As one of her contemporaries pointed out, there was a simple explanation for this dislike:

> Poor people or perfect strangers the Queen never minds meeting. It is only those she knows something about that she

does not want to encounter, as it would put her in the awkward position of either being discourteous and passing them by, or being forced to talk to them when she feels disinclined to do so. Hence out of deference to the Queen's feelings there is a tacit understanding that one must never be seen in her path. This has grown into a stereotyped rule.

The fact was that chance encounters necessitated a return to formality when she was trying to relax. 'When she passes,' reported a visiting stateman, 'we pull up and stand up uncovered etc.' To avoid this, says Fritz Ponsonby, 'we hid behind the bushes'. This, he points out, could be compromising to the dignity of distinguished visitors. Once Sir William Harcourt was out walking with Ponsonby's father when the Queen hove into sight. 'There was only a small shrub near, and Harcourt asked whether he was expected to hide behind that, but as he was six feet four inches high my father suggested that the wisest thing to do was simply to turn back.' Once as the Queen's carriage approached the Empress Eugénie was amazed to see a mad scramble of royalty trying to get out of sight. Prince Henry of Battenberg, according to one of the attendants, 'dashed off through our small private gate', while the Duke of Connaught, having 'turned appealingly to me to be shown some way out', was later seen 'madly careering down the garden'.

Yet when encounters did take place they were not nearly as bad as all this might lead one to suspect. After a drive with Henry Ponsonby at Balmoral, Sir Henry Campbell-Bannerman told his wife 'we danced a most amusing chassez-croisez with the Queen . . . the more we tried to avoid her the more she ran into us, and she passed us *three* times'. This was too much for Victoria's sense of the absurd. 'The third time the Queen laughed out loud, it was so ridiculous.'

Anyone meeting the ageing Queen in audience for the first time was increasingly liable to panic. Even a towering European figure like Bismarck was seen to be sweating profusely before his first meeting with her. (Afterwards, charmed by his reception, he was all smiles and pronounced her a 'jolly little body'.) An American diplomat noted that even valour on the battlefield was no guarantee of brave bearing in front of Queen Victoria. One valiant officer was so nervous that 'he kissed his own hand instead of that of the Queen'. Another story was told of a budding Solicitor-General who made a great spectacle of himself when receiving his knighthood:

'What am I to do?' he asked nervously of the official at the door. 'Kneel, kneel.'

Suiting the action to the word he immediately fell on his knees and, like the funny man at the child's tea party, propelled himself along the floor on his knees. Her Majesty was overcome by laughter, all the more so as, when she retreated, 'the little man followed'.

Mealtimes at Court created their own problems. As the Queen did not like loud voices, and did not think it right that subjects such as politics should be discussed in her presence, certain members of her entourage began to mumble or else maintain an agitated silence. 'So many of the Court are so *boutonné*,' complained Lady Lytton as a new lady-in-waiting in the '90s. As early as the 1840s Lady Lyttelton had noticed that the Queen had to make the running to keep mealtime conversation going. As the royal attendants became increasingly tongue-tied she had to do so all the more. Accordingly, says Fritz Ponsonby, 'when she was rather preoccupied and silent the dinner was a dismal affair, but when she was inclined to talk and interpose with witty remarks it went with a swing'.

It is difficult for an elderly lady always to be lively. One of the criticisms levelled against Queen Victoria in her old age was that her Court was 'dull'. It would indeed have been difficult for a Court presided over by someone both old and respectable to have been anything else. It is true the Queen's own tastes were simple and this led to feelings of constriction among the more sophisticated of her entourage. In later years her resident doctor complained that after a time at Balmoral 'he found himself excited about small things which when he got away he didn't care a damn for'. 'It is the funniest life conceivable: like a convent,' a Minister in Attendance confided to his wife near the end of the reign; 'We meet at meals . . . and when we have finished each is off to his cell . . .' (Greville had a similar complaint—that, apart from the Queen, there was 'very little resource or amusement' at Court—the year after her accession!) There is some evidence that at times Victoria would have liked to break the bonds. But when, for instance, she was in a relaxed mood and inclined to stay up late, according to Lady Lytton the princesses became 'fidgety'. 'Miss Phipps is often told by Princess Beatrice to interrupt the Queen and remind her it is past eleven.'

Against this background it was natural that Lady Randolph Churchill, a sensitive young woman with an American upbringing going to receive a decoration, should enter the audience chamber with some trepidation. She subsequently discovered that her trepidation was shared—by the Queen herself: 'Remarking afterwards to the lady-in-waiting that I was afraid I had been awkward and nervous, "You need not be troubled," she answered, "I know the Queen felt more shy than you did." '

Shyness, so often in royalty mistaken for stiffness or coldness, is one of the keys to understanding Queen Victoria. A Battenberg princess called it 'almost girlish bashfulness' and it can indeed be traced right back to her girlhood. She had thrashed the whole subject out with Melbourne. 'I spoke of my great nervousness, which I said I feared I would never get over.' Melbourne was honest with her: 'I won't flatter Your Majesty that you ever will.' Even at this stage she disliked the State Opening of Parliament. 'The Queen wishes they would not use such thin and slippery paper—for it is difficult to hold with nervous, and, as Lord Melbourne knows, *shaking* hands.'

During her marriage she leant heavily on Albert and her lack of confidence showed up clearly when he was not present. Undoubtedly after the Prince's death these feelings of shyness and nervousness contributed greatly to her sense of desolation and inadequacy. 'I have now been 30 years in harness,' she confessed in 1867, 'and therefore ought to know what should be—but I am *terribly shy* and nervous and *always was so*.' Still later her grand-children were to bear witness to the same phenomenon. The impression carried away by young Marie, afterwards Queen of Rumania, was not of a frightening *grande dame* but of a kindly figure, 'wee and smiling and rather shy'.

For someone who felt like this yet inspired so much awe Queen Victoria had a remarkable faculty for putting people at their ease. The young Ethel Smyth, meeting her at Balmoral, had an ex-perience shared by many: 'So awe-inspiring was the first impres-sion that I should have been terrified but for the wonderful, blue, child-like eyes, and the sweetest most entrancing smile I have ever seen on a human face.'

This smile greatly impressed Mary Waddington, the American wife of the French Ambassador. 'I watched her while she was talking and I never saw a smile make such a difference to a face. Hers is quite beautiful and lights up her whole face.' As one Victorian débutante put it, very simply, 'Queen Victoria is quite a small lady, but had such a sweet smile.'

'Certainly she had the royal art of putting people at their ease,' the later Archbishop Lang confirmed, and when amused 'her voice would break into a soft, gentle, and very delightful laugh, a sort of gurgle of pleasure'. What surprised foreigners was to find her so simple and unaffected. 'I have seldom seen so much natural-ness, simplicity, and dignity united in one personality,' declared the Prussian von Bülow. At dinner there was 'something touching in her whole bearing,' he added. 'In these moments this woman ruler of a world empire reminded me of some good old soul in Hanover, Hamburg or Holstein, as she carefully prodded the potatoes on her plate to find the softest.' Lady Lytton noticed how, on the Queen's part, she 'liked the foreign ease of manner'. This was no doubt in reaction to the over-deferential treatment she received from her own subjects. Cheerful Prince Henry of Batten-berg was a great favourite—his presence, as Victoria herself put it in one of her most vivid phrases, 'was like a bright sunbeam in my home'.

In truth, she liked people to be 'full of life and fun'. 'H.M. don't like being bored,' emphasised Sir Henry Ponsonby. She did not always manage to avoid bores. She had particular trouble with the lords-in-waiting who were political appointments made by incoming Prime Ministers. She was once moved to tell Disraeli she would 'not stand for all the *dunces* and *fools* of *rank* being thought good enough for Court'. When Gladstone was forming a new administration she got her Private Secretary to write in early: 'People she is very anxious not to have as Lords are Lord Sudeley and Lord Wrottesley—both insufferable bores.'

She had another, somewhat surprising, preference: she liked those around her to be good-looking. In how ladies looked and what they wore she took an interest strange in one who for forty years wore the fashions of 1861 and cared little about her own appearance. ('Well really,' she told her daughters when they objected to an unflattering photograph of her being hawked round the streets of London, 'I think it *very like*.') Though she disliked certain trends, such as the hair style of the 1880s ('the present fashion of fringe and frizzle in front is frightful'), normally her instinct was to approve and to congratulate pretty women on their ensemble.

With regard to male good looks and deportment, in spite of advancing years she remained highly susceptible. She liked a man to be manly, not like poor Dean Stanley, who, she was sorry to say, 'were as if he had no sex'. Young Lord Lansdowne, visiting her in '69, passed the test: 'Such a remarkably nice young man—with such good manners, and very good looking.' Nearly twenty years later, when trying to guide Gladstone over the appointment of the lords-in-waiting, Henry Ponsonby made it clear 'the Queen would like young Lord Camoys'. At the same time she was greatly impressed by the good looks of her youngest son-in-law, Henry of Battenberg. And for Prince Henry's brother, Alexander, she went overboard. 'I think him fascinating and (as in beloved Papa's case) wonderfully handsome.'

Not bad for a woman approaching seventy!

CHAPTER XV

State Occasions

For many years after the Prince Consort's death Queen Victoria avoided ceremonial occasions with all the dexterity at her command. The State Opening of Parliament, which she had never liked, she could by this stage 'only compare to an execution'. The sole source of light relief, when she felt obliged to do it, was the tempestuous entry of the House of Commons. They came in, as one observer said, 'jostling and talking like nothing on earth but a pack of schoolboys, or a herd of bullocks'—'I saw her rather smile at that.' Less formal and less exacting occasions she was better able to enjoy. She managed to perform the opening of Blackfriars Bridge without even getting out of her carriage. With a touch of her old dry humour she noted that, after the preliminary presentations, 'the bridge was considered opened, but neither I nor the Lord Mayor said so'.

From official visits by foreign heads of state she remained as far detached as possible, any unavoidable meetings taking place well away from London. She entertained the Sultan of Turkey at Osborne. A naval review was laid on, but, as she delicately put it, 'the poor Sultan was not comfortable and had to lie down a good deal below'. Still, he seemed flattered when she personally invested him with the Garter. 'I fastened the garter round him myself—and he smiled and laughed and coloured and was very much pleased.' He probably felt as much at ease as she would have done in his harem.

When the Shah of Persia was on his way to England Queen

Victoria had reason for apprehension, the Princess Royal warning her what to expect:

> The Shah of Persia always has a lamb roasted in his room which he pulls to pieces with his fingers, distributing pieces to all his ministers and attendants, all sitting on the floor . . . He also throws his pocket handkerchief across the room at his Prime Minister when he has used it, upon which this dignitary makes a profound bow and puts the handkerchief in his pocket.

Luckily, on the arrival of this somewhat unusual potentate the Prince of Wales did most of the entertaining. An official call had, however, to be paid to the Queen at Windsor where his reception must have struck him as somewhat tame. Victoria could not but see the funny side of it. 'I asked him to sit down, which we did on chairs in the middle of the room (very absurd it must have looked, and I felt very shy), my daughters sitting on the sofa.' She learned from him that he had had her *Journal of Our Life in the Highlands* translated into Persian and had read it himself. One cannot help wondering what on earth he made of it.

More to the Queen's taste than all this formality was the flow of visitors who now came to see her from distant parts of the globe. The Indian and Colonial Exhibition was rich in such exotic treats. One of the Kaffirs, she noticed approvingly, was 'a splendid man, with only a blanket draped over him, showing his fine bare legs and arms of bronze colour'. Then there were the natives of British Guiana, 'who wear in fact no clothes, but a little sort of band round their loins, the women not much more'. (Had her advisers not taken special precautions they would have shocked royal delicacy of feeling altogether by making their début stark naked.) But the African chief Cetewayo actually disappointed her by covering up. 'Unfortunately he appeared in a hideous black frock coat and trousers.'

Such visits had their amusing moments. The Indians, for instance, 'one and all, forty three in number, knelt down and kissed and stroked my feet and knees'. Two visiting Burmese chiefs were quite an embarrassment: 'They completely prostrated

15 A study in continuity. The young Queen with daughter Beatrice . . .

16 . . . and the old with grand-daughter Margaret of Connaught

17 From India to Scotland. 'God knows how much I want to be taken
care of.'

18 'H.M. don't like being bored.' High jinks among the Household
led by Alick Yorke (third from right).

themselves in front of me, and would not rise, till I at last obliged them to do so.' She saw her first game of lacrosse played by Iroquois Indians who reminded her of Hiawatha. Afterwards their chief 'read a long address in the Iroquois language, with much emphasis, having first placed a tomahawk in the ground before me, in sign of submission'. Then they 'begged to offer a basket of their manufacture to "our good mother", as they call me'. The visit to Osborne of the Chinese ambassador's wife 'with the celebrated squashed feet' was an amusing charade. 'She is by way of seeing no gentlemen,' Victoria noted drily, 'but Lord Salisbury could not help doing so, as well as everyone else on the journey.' A West African chief, says Princess Marie Louise, was another to cause a stir:

> He had been entertained at Windsor, and at the conclusion of the audience the Queen asked him whether Her Majesty could give him anything as a souvenir of his visit. The Queen, as you may remember from her photographs, always wore a very becoming widow's cap of pleated white 'lisse' with long streamers. Pointing to the cap, the Chief replied, 'Yes, Mighty Queen: I should like to have a bonnet as Your Majesty is now wearing, and I should like to be the only chief entitled to wear it. I will pass it on to my successors'.
>
> The Queen was much amused at this strange and very modest request, and at once gave the necessary order that one of her caps should be given to the Chief . . . I have been given a photograph of the Chief in full regalia, with my grandmother's cap on his head, surmounted by an ordinary top hat. The effect is quaint, to say the least.

Queen Victoria extracted every ounce of enjoyment from such strange visitors. They appealed to her in a way the drab and the ordinary never did. But this is only part of the story. When it came to the treatment of 'subject peoples', particularly those in India, some of her views were well in advance of her time. Her Viceroy, she once told Lord Salisbury,

> . . . must *hear for himself* what the feelings of the Natives really

are and not be guided by the *snobbish* and vulgar, overbearing
and offensive behaviour of our Civil and Political Agents, if we
are to go peaceably in India, and to be liked and beloved by
high and low—as well as respected—as we ought to be—and
not trying to trample on the people and continually reminding
them and making them feel they are a conquered people.

She herself was most courteous to those Indians, whether princes
or servants, who came in contact with her. She was exasperated
by the opposition within her Household to her confidential
relationship with one of her Indian attendants, the Munshi. To her
the Munshi was 'very handy and useful in many ways'—a sort of
latter-day John Brown. The Indian princes appealed more to her
romantic inclinations. At her Golden Jubilee, when she was sixty-
eight, she confessed to thinking 'the handsome young Rao of Kutch
most beautifully dressed . . . Really he and his brother were like a
dream'. All in all, had the English women who followed their
husbands out to India in the nineteenth century had Queen
Victoria's outlook the history of the British raj might have been
very different.

The Queen's Golden Jubilee was proof, if proof was needed,
that among her subjects at home she was 'liked and loved by high
and low'. Still she made no change in her outward appearance or
way of life. Though Lord Rosebery might urge that 'the symbol
of this vast Empire is a Crown not a bonnet', at the Jubilee celebrations she insisted on wearing her bonnet. Neither could she
be induced, fifty years after her accession, to celebrate the occasion
on the anniversary day. Always a stickler for such things, she
pointed to a simple fact: 'My Uncle William IV died on that day!'
When the time for celebrating did arrive there was a huge gathering of schoolchildren in Hyde Park at which, her keen ear noted,
'the children sang *God Save the Queen* somewhat out of tune'.
'The proceedings concluded by the release of a balloon bearing the
word "Victoria",' Lady Jersey remembered. 'As it ascended one
child was heard gravely explaining to another that "that was the
Queen going up to Heaven".' She was becoming a legend in her

own lifetime, but she had no intention of going up to heaven just yet.

The highlight of the last years of her reign was the Diamond Jubilee, an event unique in British history. As she drove to St. Paul's she was much moved by the 'truly marvellous' enthusiasm of the crowds though not too overcome to see the funny side: 'She supposed that the procession through London had been a very fine procession, but that she herself had been in a very bad position for seeing it.' Throughout her vast empire Jubilee celebrations went on. One of her greatest admirers celebrated in exile. Oscar Wilde, recently released from Reading Gaol and the rough justice of Victorian England, was living as 'Monsieur Melmoth' at Berneval-sur-mer. From there his friends received reports of his jubilee tea party for the local children.

> My fête was a huge success: fifteen *gamins* were entertained . . . I had a huge iced cake with *Jubilé de la Reine Victoria* in pink sugar . . . They sang the *Marseillaise* and other songs and danced a *ronde,* and also played 'God save the Queen': they said it was 'God save the Queen', and I did not like to differ from them . . . It was an amusing experience as I am hardly more than a month out of gaol.

The party, whilst establishing Wilde's popularity with the local children, nearly cost him his anonymity. As he went through the town thereafter he was followed by cries of *'Vive Monsieur Melmoth et la Reine d'Angleterre'*. Perhaps it was a fitting tribute to a man who wrote: 'Every poet should gaze at the portrait of his Queen all day long.' 'The three women I have admired most,' he wrote shortly before his death, 'are Queen Victoria, Sarah Bernhardt and Lillie Langtry—I would have married any one of them with pleasure.'

Back at home loyal Jubilee addresses were being presented, though not always with the proper degree of dignity. According to Lord Newton, the House of Commons, in its 'herd of bullocks' tradition, set a very bad example:

The Speaker in his coach—which, incidentally, sheared off a

wheel of Lord Rosebery's state coach—was followed by a hired fly containing a clerk, and the majority of M.P.s, some very badly dressed, hastening after him and dividing him from the Privy Councillors—who were in uniform and carriages—marched in disorderly procession through the Horse Guards and Mall. On arrival at the Palace they were kept penned up in a hall for a long time, and, when at last released, rushed into the ballroom, where the Speaker presented an Address aided by Balfour and Harcourt.

The Queen replied inaudibly, owing to the confusion, and I well remember her attempt to conceal her amusement at the ridiculous scene. The whole body, consisting of about 500 persons, endeavoured to retire backwards and the proceedings ended before many others had time to enter the room.

There was more decorum when the bishops came to present loyal greetings, but to no effect. As Princess Marie Louise shows, the old lady had lost none of her former antipathy for these dignitaries.

When it was all over she went on her usual afternoon drive. Edith, Lady Lytton, was in waiting and accompanied her. There was rather a prolonged silence at first, and then the Queen said, 'A very ugly party.'

Of course, black shovel hats, black gaiters, black silk aprons and the whole rather gloomy tailoring of these worthy divines was in striking contrast to the gorgeous and colourful Indian and Eastern guests she had been entertaining. Then, after a further pause, the Queen continued to express her opinion as regards the party she had described as 'very ugly'.

'I do not like bishops!'

Edith Lytton nearly fell out of the carriage in surprise and horror at the very outspoken verdict of the Queen concerning the so-called pillars of the Church. 'Oh, but your dear Majesty likes *some* bishops—for instance, the Bishop of Winchester (Randall Davidson, later Archbishop of Canterbury) and the Bishop of Ripon (Boyd Carpenter).

'Yes,' replied Her gracious Majesty, 'I like the man but *not* the Bishop.'

And this was perfectly true. She had candidly warned Davidson at the time of his elevation that, with the exception of Boyd Carpenter, she had 'never found people promoted to the Episcopate remain what they were before'. Even when she said of one of their number 'I am sure the dear bishop will go straight to Heaven when he dies', she had given John Brown full marks for his reply— 'Well, God help him when he meets John Knox.'

She had reservations, too, about some of her ministers. Liberal ministers appear to have been particularly mishap-prone. One incident, recounted by Sir Charles Petrie, involved Joseph Chamberlain during his Radical days.

It appears that one cold night while he was a member of Gladstone's administration Joe Chamberlain had to dine at Windsor, and Austen, then an undergraduate at Cambridge, lent his father a pair of old trousers to put over his Privy Councillor's breeches to keep his legs warm in the train . . .

On arriving at the Castle Chamberlain was shown into a room, for the purpose, as he supposed, of removing the superfluous nether garments. He was, therefore, in the very act of divesting himself of them when the door opened, and in walked the Queen. She had, it transpired, given orders for him to be directed to that particular apartment because she had some official business to transact with him before dinner, and a great deal of explanation was necessary before Chamberlain was able to excuse himself from the occupation in which he had been discovered.

There was a further bit of bad management at the time she was selecting Gladstone's successor. Harcourt and Rosebery were the main contenders, though Victoria was determined she would not have Harcourt. 'At some stage in the proceedings,' Rosebery's biographer relates, 'Harcourt was ushered into the Royal presence by mistake and had to be ushered out again.' A few years later when Rosebery asked her about this she laughed heartily. 'Yes, that was terrible. No one knows to this day how it happened—no one can explain it. You were not there that day—it was Mr. Gladstone that I sent for.'

In choosing Rosebery Victoria plumped for someone who was good company and amusing to talk to. Other ministers were popular for the same reason. Lord Acton, a lord-in-waiting, she was delighted to find 'light in hand and agreeable on all topics'. How much more these qualities appealed to her than Gladstonian intensity! Campbell-Bannerman was another favourite. He was both pleasant and prepared to listen to her views. Not that they always agreed. 'Sir Henry Campbell-Bannerman told me,' records Fritz Ponsonby, 'that once, when he was trying to persuade her to withdraw her opposition to some measure proposed by the Liberal Government, she said to him "I remember Lord Melbourne using the same arguments many years ago, but it was not true then and it is not true now." He said he felt like a little boy talking to his grandmother.'

Queen Victoria has been most strongly criticised for her antipathy towards Gladstone in his old age. The implication appears to be that she behaved like Elizabeth I when she ought to have emulated Elizabeth II. Jealousy, it has been suggested, was an important element in her attitude. If this was so it was certainly unconscious on her part. Her reservations began during his first administration when she began to suspect that he was trying to 'govern' her. Later it was his 'very dangerous politics' that stuck in her throat. She was not alone in her attitude. Tennyson, for instance, having once been Gladstone's friend, came to denounce what he termed 'the political decadence of Mr. Gladstone'. It was this 'decadence', together with Gladstone's increasing age and incapacity, which made her in the end consider it 'a very alarming lookout' to entrust the fate of her country to what she called 'the abominable old G. Man'.

It was not as if Gladstone himself displayed much tact. It was typical of the man that on a whistle-stop tour of Scotland he made a provocative speech at Ballater, next door to Balmoral where she was staying. She was furious. 'The Queen is *utterly* disgusted with his stump oratory—so unworthy of his position—almost under her very nose.' (In her eyes there could be no worse condemnation of a public figure than to behave 'like an American stumping orator'.) Then he was such a tremendous bore, was so intense and never knew when to stop talking. As Lady Rosebery scathingly declared, 'He will never understand a man, still less a woman.' Victoria's attempts to spare herself from his bombardment of words have a pathetic air about them. 'But he must be *really* quiet,' she suggested hopefully to him when he was advised to cut his work-load, 'and not occupy himself at *all* with affairs and not write long letters like the one he did yesterday.' Vain hope. Unfortunately for Gladstone Queen Victoria was incapable of simulating feelings she did not have. In consequence, when he came to form his last administration he complained that his audience was 'such as took place between Marie Antoinette and her executioner'.

This antipathy between Queen and statesman was not public knowledge at the time, though well understood in the Royal Household. A story about it was even whispered round London society in the 1880s. Though denied at the time it did full justice to the Queen's sentiments. It arose out of the antics of one of the Maids of Honour: having danced before her mistress, she provoked royal laughter by Salome-like demanding Gladstone's head on a charger. There was, says Elizabeth Longford, further anti-Gladstonian mirth in church where it was more difficult to give way:

> An appeal to the Almighty in Crathie Church by wee Dr. MacGregor to 'send down His wisdom on the Queen's Meenisters who sorely needed it', created havoc in the royal pew. Queen Victoria went purple with suppressed laughter and her lady-in-waiting, Lady Antrim, could not resist a half-audible 'Amen'.

To be fair to Queen Victoria, her granddaughter Princess Alice reveals that the old lady was equally convulsed when she herself was the subject of presbyterian exhortations at Crathie:

It was here on one famous occasion that a certain minister made a lengthy prayer for Grandmama Victoria which ended up with 'and that she may skip like a he-goat upon the mountains'—words that I could never forget. It was noticed afterwards how Grandmama was deeply moved by the prayer and buried her face in her hands.

CHAPTER XVI

Command Performance

She was now an old lady. Yet at seventy-one, as at seventeen, the terpsichorean urges were strong.

> After dinner, the other ladies and gentlemen joined us in the Drawing-room and we pushed the furniture back and had a nice little impromptu dance, Curtis's band being *entraînant*. We had a quadrille, in which I danced with Eddy!! It did quite well, then followed some waltzes and polkas.

As if to demonstrate her interest she had a new ballroom installed at Balmoral. Not that all her associates shared her enthusiasm, particularly as regards Scottish dancing. As his son recalled, Henry Ponsonby for one had distinct reservations.

> As the years passed Ponsonby became doubtful not only of the necessity but of the desirability of her indulging with such zeal in dancing reels. Yet as late as 1891, when she was seventy-two at an informal dance in the Castle drawing-room, he was obliged to admit: 'The Queen danced with Prince Henry; light airy steps in the old courtly fashion; no limp or stick but every figure carefully and prettily danced.' But the usual gillies' ball was a rough-and-tumble affair with a great deal of shouting and she never missed it.

Her energy in her early seventies was indeed remarkable. 'The Queen to my intense astonishment,' gasped Marie Mallet, 'ascended a huge ladder to mount a horse twenty-six years old which pranced along quite gaily.' Increasingly, though, she had to confine herself to spectator activities. One of these—and one more sign that she was returning to the habits of her married life—was watching *tableaux vivants*. Just as the young Vicky years ago had been Summer in *The Seasons*, so now the matronly Beatrice would appear as Queen Elizabeth, or as India in a tableau representing *Empire*. Victoria could not see enough of such spectacles.

Although she never went to a public theatre after the death of the Prince Consort she occasionally went out to other forms of entertainment. In 1886 she told Henry Ponsonby with obvious pride that, having already been twice to the Albert Hall since its opening, she 'went today to hear Gounod's splendid music and Albani's glorious singing'. A few years later, writing more like a young girl pleading with her father than a queen in her seventies, she asked:

> Does Sir Henry think it possible for her to go privately to see *Venice?* She hears it is admirably done . . . In the day of course and it is not a theatre or a play and it will be 5 months and ½ after her dear grandson's death and 3½ after her dear son-in-law's and she would very much like to see it.

Usually, though, she preferred her entertainment at home. Music remained high on her list as a source of pleasure. At Balmoral Sir Henry Campbell-Bannerman was struck by her enjoyment of the music from the new Italian operas—even when the players were more English than they pretended to be:

> Curtis's band played in the corridor every evening and H.M. was rather concerned when he spoke approvingly of their 'Viennese trio,' for she thought they were all English, but was reassured on learning that their address was in Kentish Town. 'The Queen asks for one thing after another—*Cavelleria* twice—and "quite charming, so *beautiful*".'

C-B agreed and pocketed the card of 'Mr. Curt von Kentish Town', as he dubbed him, for future use.

At other times more highbrow performers were engaged. Grieg and Paderewski came to Windsor to play for her, and she even heard the young Pablo Casals. As her enthusiasm mounted increasingly ambitious concerts were organised for her and the Waterloo Chamber at Windsor was brought into use. When, in 1889, Albani came down with the de Reszke brothers, the Queen's pleasure was intense:

> The duet from *Lohengrin*, which is quite a long scene, was beyond anything beautiful, so dramatic, and Albani almost acted it. She was in great force. The music lasted till four, and I could have listened to it much longer. It was indeed a treat.

Albani's 'almost acting' was an uncanny presage of even greater treats to come. When Victoria paid a visit to the Prince of Wales at Sandringham in 1889 he had the ballroom converted into a theatre and brought a full professional cast down from London headed by Henry Irving and Ellen Terry. The Queen's excited account of the performance shows how fully it rekindled her old love of the theatre.

> The stage was beautifully arranged and with great scenic effects, and the pieces were splendidly mounted and with numbers of people taking part . . . The piece, *The Bells*, is a melodrama and is very thrilling. The hero (Irving), though a mannerist of the Macready type, acted wonderfully. He is a murderer, and frequently imagines he hears the bells of the horses in the sledge, in which sat the Polish Jew, who is murdered. The way in which Irving acted his own dream, and describes the way in which he carried out the murder, is wonderful and ghastly, as well as the scene at his death. He had carried his secret about with him for thirteen years! . . . it was a most successful performance.

So successful was it that the Queen began herself to bring London companies down to Windsor. Irving and Ellen Terry started things off successfully with Tennyson's *Becket*. Later Eleanora Duse performed in *La Locandiera*. 'Admirable' thought the Queen. The *Comédie Française* company were still more entertaining with 'some most amusing monologues, so witty and clever, without the least vulgarity'. 'There is,' she admitted, 'nothing like the French for doing that kind of thing.' George Grossmith in *How Ladies of the Future will make Love* was also exceedingly funny. Truth to tell the old Queen, like the young, preferred something that made her laugh, or else a 'thrilling' drama, to anything very deep.

On a still more ambitious level the operatic possibilities of the Waterloo Gallery were tried out. As Fritz Ponsonby testified, pitfalls were present for the unwary:

> The acoustics were not really good for opera, and the singers usually came down early to try their voices. One of the difficulties was that the Queen sat herself in the front row within a few feet of the singers. When Francisco Tamagno came down to sing in one opera he arrived very late and had no time to try his voice. The result was that he nearly blew the Queen's cap off when he let himself go.

Even worse, Plunket Greene actually believed her to be deaf. As a result his rendering of *Strike him dead* 'nearly blew the Queen out of her chair'.

Starting the ball rolling the full Savoy company came down to give a performance of *The Gondoliers*. It was a huge success. The Queen thought the opera 'quite charming' and Gilbert's dialogue 'very amusing'. But in the field of grand opera she was in her seventh heaven. 'I had not heard an Italian opera for thirty-one years,' she wrote in November 1891 after a performance of *Cavelleria Rusticana* which she found 'most pathetic and touching beyond words'. 'The whole performance was a great success and I love the music which is so melodious and characteristically Italian.' Other operas followed, among them *Il Trovatore* (her birthday 'treat' one year), Gounod's *Faust* ('the music is heavenly'), and *Carmen*. She first saw *Carmen* produced in 1892. It was 'brilliant, gay, and exciting, with lovely music which I know well'. She did not, however, know the plot, as her grand-daughter Marie, sitting next to her 'almost childlike, pleasurably excited' grandmama, discovered.

I noticed that Grandmama was not only following the music with keen interest, but also the plot of the play. Somewhat bewildered by the passionate story, she kept asking me questions, which were not easy to answer owing to the loudness of the music and the unequal height of our chairs . . . The first act over she turned to me for fuller explanations about the story. With a very young woman's diffidence I tried to impart to my grandparent my knowledge of Carmen's rather wild tale. Grandmama's smile broadened, this was the sort of story that did not often reach her ears . . .

Leaning towards me, her eyes full of dawning comprehension, she nevertheless pressed me for further explanations which, with flaming cheeks, I give as best I can. Grandmama raised her fan over her face, she is delightfully, pleasurably scandalised, but she understands; leaning towards me, her fan still over her mouth, she whispers: 'But, oh my dear child, I am afraid she's really not very nice!'

This engaging maidenly coyness was still with the Queen when she was eighty. *Messaline* had just been produced in London when Bernard Mallet noted in his diary:

Marie says the Queen is wonderfully well and keen. Perhaps memory not quite what it was. She is in excellent spirits and full of jokes. Horrified at 'Messaline' and made Marie read all the criticisms. It ought never to have been licensed, she says. She was very funny at the evening concert about it, as she told Marie, 'I spoke to Signor Tosti about it—and put my fan quite over my face', as, indeed, Marie observed her doing. It is delightfully young, modest and naive!

Tosti's services were drawn on when the Queen wished to hear distinguished artists. Whoever her visitors were, they were assured of an enthusiastic reception. Whether Albani, Clara Butt, Irving or Ellen Terry, 'her manner to the radiant artists was perfect', declared Lady Lytton. Irving, though an actor, was, as the Queen said, 'a gentleman as so many are now'. When she set the seal to the respectability of the theatre by knighting him she dropped her normal custom of not speaking during the ceremony. 'I am very, very pleased,' she told him. As if to reciprocate, Ellen Terry paid Queen Victoria one of the finest compliments a great actress could pay another woman. The Queen's voice, she later recalled, was 'like a silver stream flowing over golden stones'. (In Victoria's youth Fanny Kemble had been equally impressed: 'The Queen's voice is exquisite, nor have I ever heard any spoken words more musical.')

Occasional visits by professional companies proved insufficient to satisfy the new-found royal appetite for things theatrical. Victoria secured extra enjoyment by encouraging members of her family and Household to put on amateur productions, and in order to obtain still more pleasure she would frequently turn up at the rehearsals. 'Everyone seemed much pleased,' wrote Arthur Bigge after one production, 'but none more so than H.M. who has extracted the maximum amount of fun and interest out of the fortnight's preparation.' Some of her more blasé descendants wondered at an old lady's ability to be so easily amused by 'tiresome theatricals'. 'It is extraordinary how pleased Grandma is with such small things, for she is quite childish in some ways about them,' complained Prince Albert Victor. Nor did man-of-the-world Campbell-Bannerman care much for having to see both the dress rehearsal and the actual production of what turned out to be 'our old friend *Pattes de Mouche* watered down into *A Scrap of Paper*.' (Afterwards he had her 'with her face puckered up and laughing' when he described the more earthy Paris production.)

Nevertheless, these amateur efforts appear to have reached quite a high standard. Ronald Sutherland Gower, who saw Tom Taylor's *Helping Hands* performed at Osborne, thought it 'admirably acted'. The Queen was certainly impressed—'I was near enough to see with what zest the Queen entered into the fun of the piece.' Without a doubt Alick Yorke's acting and organising abilities helped things to go with a swing; while the younger princesses also entered into the spirit of the thing.

An insight into one production is afforded by the experience of the Princess Royal's daughter, young Vicky. To help take her mind off an unhappy love affair she was invited to stay with her grandmother and encouraged to join in the theatricals. As the Queen explained to the Princess Royal, half apologetically and half reassuringly, the play chosen was really a 'very *proper* and *very innocent* little piece'. 'After dinner Vicky, Mr. Yorke and Ethel C[adogan] acted a little, most ridiculous little piece called *Caught at Last*. Vicky and Mr. Yorke did the chief parts . . .They did it so well. We were kept in fits of laughter.' As young Vicky told her mother, 'no-one enjoyed it more than the Queen. I heard her laugh heartily many a time during the piece.' The old lady enjoyed it so much in fact that next day she arranged a repeat performance which 'went better than ever'.

As well as extracting the maximum enjoyment from both rehearsals and actual productions the Queen took a keen interest in the plots and language of the plays. With her dislike of vulgarity and indelicacy she did not hesitate to make alterations where it suited her. Since most of these amateur productions were already English variations on the original French plays additional changes could, Arthur Ponsonby discovered, lead to ridiculous situations:

The play was a translation of a French piece called *L'Homme Blasé*. When the cast was made up but before they knew their parts the Queen bade them perform before her. She was amused; but finding that Princess Beatrice who had a good part in the first act did not come on again, she ordered Colonel Collins to re-write the last act so that she might re-appear. On this Major Bigge writes: 'I think Collins ought to have added to the printed description in the Programme: *The return and reconciliation of Mrs. Ironbrace is by command!*'

To begin with, the marriages in the acted version were an insertion. In the original French there were none! This much amused the Empress Eugénie who was present.

The mixing of members of the Household with younger members of the Royal Family, under the Queen's eagle eye, could lead to additional complications, as Fritz Ponsonby found to his discomfort when rehearsing *She Stoops to Conquer*.

. . . Arthur Bigge and I did the two lovers and Princess Louise and Princess Beatrice the two principal ladies' parts. The Queen came to the rehearsals, which frightened us all very much, and when she saw me chucking Princess Louise under the chin (I was supposed to mistake her for a barmaid) she thought this was overdone. I received a message that I had better not indulge in any chucking under the chin. The next day I went through my part but never came within touching distance of Princess Louise, and again received a message to say that I was overdoing it the other way. I consulted Princess Louise herself, who roared with laughter at my dilemma, and we finally hit off a happy medium.

But Arthur Bigge, in *L'Homme Blasé*, found himself in an even worse dilemma:

The result of the rehearsal is that H.M. thinks I had better not call her daughter 'a degraded woman' and I agree! Also she is *not* to say to Sir C. in describing her wooing of Clutterbuck 'I have nothing to offer as dowry but my virtue,' to which C. replies 'Ah, little enough!'

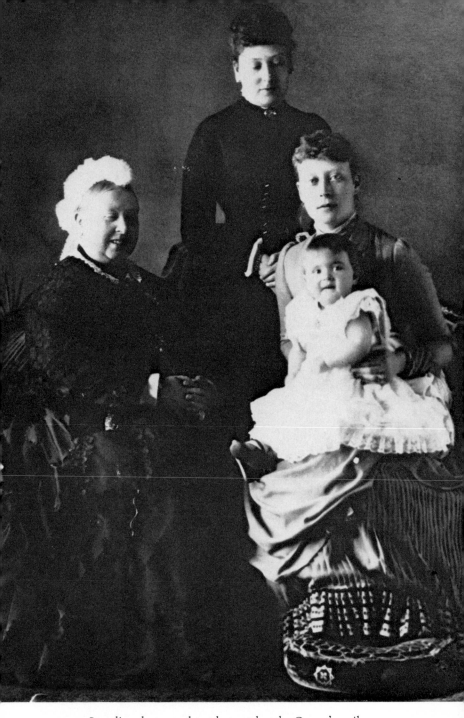

19 Speedier photography at last catches the Queen's smile

20 The smile caught outdoors. 'I never saw a smile make such a difference to a face.'

21 'No one ever remembered such cloudy days.'

CHAPTER XVII

Gangan

Inside the old Queen's mind there still seemed to be a little girl longing to get out. Luckily for this side of her, her declining years were filled with a never-ending array of grandchildren and great-grandchildren. Their presence brought a joyful new dimension to her life. No longer were there allusions to the breeding habits of the rabbits in Windsor Park. 'Now,' says one of her grand-daughters, 'she showed the proverbial grandmother's lenience . . . she was "Gangan" whom they could coax and wheedle.'

Though occasionally she tried to live up to her old principle of not spoiling the young, her efforts became increasingly ineffectual. True she once made an attempt to be firm with Beatrice's eldest boy when he wrote home from Wellington College asking for more pocket-money. No, she told him, you must try and live within your allowance. All to no avail. No need to worry, came his reply, all was now well: he had sold his grandmother's letter to another boy for thirty shillings.

Lady Lytton, riding in the Queen's carriage at Balmoral, was surprised at just how relaxed the children were with the old lady.

We had tea by the bridge of Dee and the Grand Duchess [of Hesse, an older granddaughter] and Princess Ena [a younger one] who were riding met us there, and there was much chaff and no stiffness. We had passed the little four-year-old Princess [Elizabeth of Hesse, a great-granddaughter] in a pony carriage, and she said 'Thank you dear Granma for lending me these ponies,' and offered the Queen a peppermint which she took and enjoyed.

There was a similar lack of formality, as Victoria herself was pleased to observe, on the part of her great-grandson David, the future King Edward VIII. 'He always tries at luncheon time to pull me up out of my chair, saying, "Get up, Gangan," and then to one of the Indian servants, "Man pull it," which makes us laugh very much.'

As birthdays remorselessly came round and her grandchildren joined in the celebrations she had to confess that she had lost her former desire to join Albert at the earliest opportunity.

Balmoral 24th May 1893—My poor old birthday, my seventy-fourth. I wish now it was instead sixty-fourth. We dined fifteen, all the Household. There was a very nice surprise after-wards. A small stage had been erected in the Drawing-room and five charming tableaux were performed by my grand-children . . . The subjects were: Little Red Ridinghood, Jack and Jill, Cinderella, Mother Hubbard's Tale and Grandmama's Birthday. Grandmama's Birthday almost brought tears to my eyes. Sandra looked so nice with a grey wig, wearing one of my caps and Leopold in her arms. The whole was so prettily arranged and gave me great pleasure.

Having small children about the place—Beatrice's four children lived with her all the time—also meant noise and disturbance. 'Her private apartments,' noted one observer, 'are never free from their childish raids, nor from the litter of a most miscellaneous collection of toys' whilst the imposing Grand Corridor at Windsor Castle 'generally contains a large hair-covered horse which is dragged up and down'. Such distractions did not bother Victoria.

No prattle, however noisy, disturbs her, no romping, however rough, causes her dismay. The Princess Ena rushes up and down the corridors, pulling behind her one of her tiny brothers, mounted upon a wooden steed. But although the hearts of the servants jump into their mouths as they perceive the imminent risk of disaster to which priceless objects adorning the apart-ments are liable, the grandchildren are never checked. And if Prince Alexander springs upon the back of the Queen's draught-ass, in order to test his abilities as a bareback rider, he is not restrained.

Her attitude was 'I love these darling children so, almost as much as their own parents.'

She tried to make other people's children feel equally at home. Mary Gladstone, when she took her young daughter to see her, was touched by the tenderness with which the old lady treated the child, asking her simple questions and kissing her repeatedly. (Forty years earlier a previous generation of Gladstones had met with the same warm welcome, encouraged to play, been well kissed and given a woolly lamb to take home.) One village boy who grew up near Windsor also had happy memories of her. When she saw children playing while out for her drive, he said, 'the Queen would always smile and say a few words to us, then pat the head of the nearest. On several occasions that was me.' *The Notebooks of a Spinster Lady* for 1892 had its own story to tell:

> Lunching with Lady Westbury sat next to Mrs. N. whose children are rather intimate in the royal nurseries, and were sent for the other day to see the Queen dressed for the Drawing-room. They waited in the ward-room (whatever that may be) with the two little Battenberg children and the two little Albanys. The little Battenbergs seem very much at home with their Granny, and ran up to her with 'O Gangan! You said we could come to see you dressed!' 'Well,' said the Queen, 'you see I have come to see you instead. Now have a good look!' And she walked up and down before them, turning about so they might see her well, and not forgetting to order sponge cake and milk for her little guests before she went off to hold her more stately reception.

That she had not lost her old gift of putting children at their ease was borne out when she first met Marie Mallet's tiny son Victor, one of her many godchildren. His visit to Court when he was less than two years old got off to a bad start: he mistook the formidable Duchess of Roxburghe for the Queen and burst into tears. Once in the royal presence, however, Marie was relieved to find that everything went swimmingly. '. . . I said to Victor "What do you say? This is the Queen." He promptly kissed her hand and answered clearly "Good morning, Queen" charmed at once by the Queen's beaming smile and great gentleness of voice and manner.' On his next visit, as Marie told her husband, he was quite at his ease.

> . . . he kissed the Queen's hand twice in the most courtier-like manner and answered all her questions quite promptly telling Her Majesty you were at your office and that you rode a 'flying machine'. The Queen said, 'I suppose you mean a bicycle, dear?' upon which he answered in shrill tones, 'Nanny says it is a flying machine' which made her laugh heartily. Then Her Majesty said 'Do you know who I am?' 'Keenie' replied he quite loud and decided.

A year later, to his godmother's delight, young Victor was more relaxed than ever. 'He introduced a comic element by suddenly producing a small but beloved black pig which he had insisted on bringing from London and said rather loudly, "Look at this pig, I have brought it all the way from London to see you." The Queen laughed till she cried . . .'

Not all grown-ups realised how easily children amused her. Lord Kilmarnock was so embarrassed when he discovered his young son had sent her a letter that he immediately dispatched an apology. 'Pray tell Lord Kilmarnock,' she instructed her Private Secretary, 'that the Queen was delighted with the little letter of his little boy, as nothing pleases her more than the artless kindness of little children. She has written him an answer and posted it to him.' The future Lord Ernle knew his monarch better and when invited to Osborne he asked his little daughter whether she had any message for the Queen. 'Oh, yes,' said the child, 'ask her to give me the little mouse that lives under her chair.' This message was duly delivered and could not have met with a better response.

> Not only did she laugh heartily at the story, but she called up several of the guests and insisted on my telling it again. The

last to be called up was a rather elderly peer, who evidently did not see the point of the story. The Queen turned
upon him with indignation and said, 'What Lord —, don't
you know

> Pussy-cat, pussy-cat, where have you been?
> I've been to London to see the great Queen.
> Pussy-cat, pussy-cat, what saw you there?
> I saw the little mouse under her chair.'

In addition to their naturalness and the occasional amusing
incident the old Queen obtained another bonus from her association with children. She was able on their behalf to arrange juvenile
entertainments which she then enjoyed at least as much as they
did. Thus, when she was nearly seventy, Hengler's Circus was
brought to the Riding School at Windsor, ostensibly for the third
birthday of Prince Leopold's daughter. It was the first time
Victoria had seen a circus since Albert's death. She was happy to
discover that she was still as fascinated by performing animals as
she had been in the days of Van Amburgh's lions half a century
before. Thereafter she never missed a similar opportunity. When
the American Exhibition was at Earl's Court she took her grandchildren along and found Buffalo Bill's Wild West 'a very extraordinary and interesting sight'. Lord Ronald Sutherland Gower
witnessed her enthusiasm.

> Some of us went in the Deadwood Coach, which driven at a
> great rate round the arena, is attacked by mounted Indians,
> and much firing takes place from within and outside the vehicle.
> The Queen seemed delighted with the performance; she looked
> radiant. At the close of the performance Buffalo Bill, at Her
> Majesty's desire, was presented, as well as the Indian Chief,
> 'Red Skin', and two of the Squaws with their 'papooses' whose
> little painted faces the Queen stroked.

Once, at Balmoral, she heard that Pindar's Circus, very much
down on its luck, was camping on Ballater Moor. It was immediately summoned to give a royal performance by the Dee and

the local people were invited to attend. The Queen watched it from her carriage. It was noticed how she 'sat through the two hours' performance, apparently with as much enjoyment as the children'.

She first saw the circus of the self-styled Lord George Sanger in 1898. On this occasion Sanger himself was unable to attend. The following year, when the Queen was eighty, Sanger was told she would like a repeat performance. This time he arranged to be present, though he had cause to wonder what the fount of honour might say to a trumped-up 'lord'. (There was a persistent rumour among Victorian children that Queen Victoria had given him the title 'in return for being allowed to put her head inside the jaws of one of his best lions'.) With this thought at the back of his mind Sanger arranged the best possible performance:

> I went to Windsor, and in the courtyard of the castle paraded my show, with every adjunct of embellishment I could think of . . . The Queen watched the spectacle from her carriage, and liked it so well she had the parade repeated. When it was over Sir Arthur Bigge came to me and said Her Majesty desired I should be presented to her. Then he led me to the Royal Carriage, and as I bowed low, said: 'Your Majesty, this is Mr. Sanger.'
>
> In a voice singularly high, clear, and penetrating, the Queen said: 'So you are Mr. Sanger?'
>
> 'Yes, Your Majesty,' I replied.
>
> Then, with a smile and a twinkle in those steadfast eyes: '*Lord* George Sanger, I believe?'
>
> This, with the accent on the '*Lord*', was distinctly embarrassing, but I managed to stammer out: 'Yes, if Your Majesty pleases!'
>
> 'It is very amusing,' was the royal lady's answer, 'and I gather you have borne the title very honourably!'

She went on to ask 'a whole fire of questions about my circus and the animals, particularly the elephants, in which Her Majesty took a great interest'. The following year, when his elephants were involved in an accident, she made detailed enquiries, wanting to know the names of the animals involved.

The child-like interest she took in performing animals did not meet with universal approval, as when one newspaper criticised her for stopping her carriage to watch a performing bear—just as she had enjoyed watching Van Amburgh's lions so many years ago. Another complaint was voiced by one of the Court Ladies— 'We have been enjoying a fourth-rate Circus this afternoon much less than the Queen.' Little did this Lady realise that she was repeating the cry from the heart uttered by previous ladies-in-waiting over forty years before. But the old Queen was as incorrigible as the young one. One of her servants listed some of the 'very promiscuous entertainers' she continued to summon to Windsor Castle ostensibly to entertain her grandchildren:

> On one occasion a pair of dancing bears was enthusiastically applauded, while another time, a 'Punch and Judy' gave intense pleasure to the Queen. Once the little Princess Ena caught sight of a monkey in Windsor Town, and the owner thereof was, with his barrel organ and animal, immediately summoned to play in the Quadrangle beneath the windows of the Oak Dining-room. The Queen was much amused when the monkey climbed the portico and tried to find a way into the Castle through the dining-room windows.

Russell Thorndike as a schoolboy at Windsor remembered Queen Victoria attending school plays, anxious to see the children enjoying themselves. One of his most vivid recollections was of her keen appreciation of the barrel organ, which was turned between the acts. Her granddaughter Vicky, writing home from Balmoral, confirmed the royal taste. 'Yesterday after lunch,' she told her mother, 'I turned one of those delightful "turning-organs"— Grandmama delights in them.' There was even a New Year dance one year with music provided by the barrel organ.

'It is,' one of her loyal subjects suggested, 'with such simple pastimes as these homely amusements, about which the great public never hear, that our beloved Sovereign has preserved her young heart and cheerful disposition.' Perhaps so. But it is also against this background that can best be savoured the famous story of the Victorian lady who had just witnessed Sarah Bernhardt giving one of her highly passionate performances as Cleopatra. The lady then turned to a companion and uttered the understatement of the century: 'How different, how *very* different, from the home life of our own dear Queen!'

Not that simple tastes and delight in childish things meant that in old age her mind lost its former acuteness. Indeed as regards her sense of humour if any change can be discerned as she advanced towards her eighties it is an increasing dryness and a greater aptitude for repartee. Little incidents would spark her off, as Marie Mallet found during a visit to a zoo near Nice.

> The Queen paid a visit to the Zoo Garden near here, belonging to a certain Comtesse de la Grange, '*ci-devant cocotte*', and was presented with a new-laid ostrich egg; this was carefully blown by the chef and its contents manufactured into an omelette which Her Majesty pronounced delicious.
>
> On the egg the doubtful Comtesse had scrawled her name. 'Just as if she had laid it herself,' remarked the Queen.

Fritz Ponsonby too remembered her little sly looks and the apt comments that would accompany them. When a visiting clergyman said that in the East End of London he had been in a house where seven people slept in one bed, 'the Queen dryly remarked, "Had I been one of them I would have slept on the floor."' When it seemed likely that the arrival of a group of visitors would lead to a shortage of rooms at Balmoral her Household were staggered to hear her say, 'No room? Then we must double up, that's all.' 'I did not,' commented Ponsonby, 'grasp whether the Queen intended to take part in this unpleasant manoeuvre.'

As she grew older some of her expressions became so old fashioned as to cause amusement among the younger generation. Her young granddaughters were much taken with her admonition about 'junketing'—'Remember, your dear Grandpapa disliked the Princesses junketing with members of the Household.'

One peculiarity she retained throughout her life was her use of the word 'news' as if it were plural. On the eve of her accession she had observed that 'the news of the King are so very bad'. In her middle years on hearing of Lincoln's assassination she was moved to remark: 'These American news are most dreadful and awful—one never heard of such a thing—I only hope it will not be *catching elsewhere.*' After Gordon's death at Khartoum her famous telegram to Gladstone declared 'these news from Khartoum are frightful'. On one occasion there were 'two horrible news' which made her feel 'quite overcome'.

To modern ears her descriptions of the journeys she made in what she called her 'rolling chair'—the wheelchair she used in later life—create mental pictures certainly not intended. 'I had to be rolled over into the breakfast room . . . Was rolled over into the Green drawing-room . . . Was rolled over to the Middle-room looking down the Mall . . .' When she gave a tea party for soldiers' families during the Boer War her Journal contained the startling entry 'I was rolled up and down round the table.'

No one, however, could express herself more forcefully than Queen Victoria even in old age. 'Horrid,' 'frightful', 'disgusting' and 'dreadful' were adjectives with which she continued to pepper her outpourings of indignation. 'Those *horrid* Bulgarians!' was the expression remembered by a Foreign Office official as typifying her marginal comments on despatches. Her expressions could be remarkably vivid. She once described a bishop in poor health as 'very transparent' and the Prince Imperial as 'rather short and stumpy'. Lord Granville, she decided, was 'a very weak reed to lean on'—'he is as weak and sweet as rose water'.

Her mode of speaking, besides its clarity, was remarkable for its emphasis. A conversation recorded by the first Lord Russell of Liverpool shows that her habit of emphasising words was present in her speech as well as her writing. She was criticising a Highland family some of whose land she rented. 'I don't like the — s . . . because they are *very bad* to their tenants,' she declared, 'and many of their cottages are in a *horrid state* . . . I am a tenant *myself* . . . and I have made *many* improvements, and *every time* I have made an improvement my rent has been raised.' Such verbal exuberance helped compensate for grammar that was imperfect and spelling that occasionally left something to be desired. 'Schocking' and 'holly days' had been among her youthful errors. 'Bewhildering' was a word that long continued to bewilder her. 'Crisises' kept occurring through the years. Now and again she got confused with her metaphors, as when, annoyed with Gladstone, she suggested it would be a good idea to 'take the sails out of the abominable old G. Man'. And when anxious to minimise the damage caused by the incendiary statements of her grandson the Kaiser, she asked Lord Salisbury 'to do all you can to pour oil on the flames'.

By and large her treatment of the Kaiser, whom privately she thought 'far too spoilt', was eminently sensible. It would not do to give him 'a good snub', she told the Prince of Wales—'Those sharp cutting answers only irritate and do harm'. Though not above giving him 'a piece of my mind', she tried not to take his posturings too seriously. His birthday present to her one year, she told his mother, was 'as usual very funnily inscribed'. His message ran: 'May God preserve our revered belovedest Colleague for the benefit of Europe, its nations and their peace'. 'I think the colleague will amuse you,' suggested his grandmother.

The Kaiser was at least understandable, whereas American jargon and American manners were beyond her. She could not comprehend how President Grant's wife during an audience 'in her funny American way' could refer to her son as 'our pet'. After meeting a new American ambassador she remarked, as if stating a contradiction, 'Mr. Bayard is very American, but very civil and kind'. American journalese she found incomprehensible. When Prince Leopold and Princess Louise visited New York, says Leopold's daughter,

. . . one newspaper published a long article of welcome under the heavy type heading of 'VIC'S CHICKS.' Now it happened that my father had a terrier named 'Vic' and when he sent the article to Queen Victoria she either failed to understand the journalistic jargon or thought it in bad taste and was 'not amused'. 'How odd of them,' she wrote to Papa with some acidity, 'to mention your dog.'

Her own Court was sometimes in receipt of even odder messages from Victoria herself. Fritz Ponsonby, for instance, once sought to prove to one of the other Gentlemen that the statues in the entrance hall at Osborne were on pivots. He ended up with an enormous statue of Psyche in his arms and, though he managed to set it down without it smashing to pieces, one wing was chipped and eventually a crane had to be used to hoist it back into position. Feeling, as he said, 'like a housemaid confessing to a broken teacup', he asked Princess Beatrice to explain to the Queen what had happened.

Princess Beatrice told me after dinner that the Queen had quite understood it was an accident, but intended to send a message to all the Household that 'they must not touch the statues and certainly not play with them'. This message was duly conveyed to all the ladies and gentlemen, but Lady Lytton, who had not heard about my accident, was mystified at receiving a message that in future she was not to touch the statues and certainly not to play with them. . . .

As the Queen advanced in years she became, like old people generally, increasingly prone to talk about her youth. The Ponsonbys, says Arthur, knew her well in this mood:

She liked relating reminiscences of the past: how she once took up a fork at a ball supper in mistake for her fan and walked into the ballroom with it: 'Not so bad as poor dear Mama who took the snuffers for her pocket handkerchief and went out walking with them.'

On another occasion she said she remembered seeing George III's statue going down the Long Walk at Snow Hill in 1829 and asked me why there was no inscription. I said, yes there was, in Latin, 'To the best of Fathers' by George IV. The Queen laughed. 'The best of Fathers! Why, they never spoke!'

In her old age, a flood of stories appeared about her early life—how at her accession, for example, Carlyle had declared: 'Poor little Queen, she is at an age when a girl can hardly be trusted to choose a bonnet for herself: yet a task has been laid upon her from which an archangel might shrink.' 'Very amusing,' she thought. She was less amused by the publication of Greville's revelations of her 'wicked uncles'—'like Judas writing the lives of the Apostles' as one reader put it. It was her habit, though, to look charitably on earlier times, for, as she once explained, 'in those days even the best people were excessively coarse'.

Her memory remained excellent and her honesty as intense as ever. When she heard that Sir William Harcourt had purchased a Landseer portrait of her to prevent its export to America (a traffic in such things existed even in those days) she sent him a message: 'Her Majesty hopes you will not think she ever wore her hair as Landseer has represented it. He insisted on placing it so for artistic reasons, but much against her will.' Was it true, she was asked that on the day of her accession Lord Melbourne (of all people!) had opened the Bible and read to her from the Book of Kings? What an idea! 'From beginning to end it is a *complete invention*, and the Queen *never heard* of it even . . .' Oscar Wilde asked permission to publish any verses she had written. 'Really, what will people not say and invent,' she exclaimed, 'Never could the Queen in her whole life write *one line of poetry* serious or comic or make a line even.' She had already put Tennyson right on this score. 'Every one can write verses,' he had said in his vague way, 'I dare say Your Majesty can.' 'No, that I cannot,' was her honest rejoinder, 'I never could make two lines meet in my life.'

In order to give herself greater freedom of expression she resorted increasingly in old age to what the Household called 'Ladies' Dinners'. Only ladies were present and the minimum of formality observed throughout the evening. On these occasions, says Lady Ponsonby, the old Queen would be amused 'almost beyond endurance till she was simply breathless and could bear no more'. Basically she had not changed much from the days when Creevey had observed her to be 'a homely little thing *when she is at her ease*, and she is evidently dying to be always more so'. She still liked cheerful companions, though not all the Court ladies of her later years were as light-hearted as she would have wished. Lady Erroll, for instance, was a keen advocate of Temperance and Sunday Observance. On neither subject could the Queen agree with her. 'Dear Lady Erroll's evangelistic efforts,' reported Marie Mallet, 'culminated in the presentation to Lord Cross of a tract on temperance! He related this last night to the Queen at dinner amid shouts of laughter. I never saw the Queen more amused.' After the death of Princess Beatrice's husband, according to Princess Marie Louise, Lady Erroll was equally off-beam:

> . . . the Queen was at Osborne and she went for her customary drive with Lady Erroll, who was then in waiting. These dear elderly ladies, swathed in crepe, drove in an open carriage, called a sociable. The Queen was very silent, and Leila (Lady Erroll) thought it time to make a little conversation. So she said, 'Oh, Your Majesty, think of when we shall meet our dear ones again in Heaven!'
> 'Yes,' said the Queen.
> 'We shall all meet in Abraham's bosom,' said Leila.
> 'I will *not* meet Abraham,' said the Queen.

Evidently she had a pretty poor opinion of that somewhat un-Victorian patriarch. In any case, according to Sir James Reid, Leila's religious endeavours would have been better employed at home:

> He used to relate how Lord Erroll read prayers every day sometimes with comments as if he were thinking. One day he read in the lessons 'It is easier for a camel to go through the eye of a needle than for a rich man, etc.', on which he exclaimed, 'Oh, that's damned nonsense. Let us pray.'

Far from becoming more puritanical as she grew older the Queen fully retained her old broad sense of humour. She still had a taste for the occasional risqué story. Once Fritz Ponsonby, conversing at dinner with a French visitor, was taken aback by her intervention.

The Queen was in a charming and fascinating mood and she soon chipped in to our French conversation and was very witty and amusing. She suddenly broke into English and laughed so much I thought she would have a fit. I had written out a memorandum in which her approval was asked for the Royal Irish Fusiliers to wear a green hackle in their busbies. Instead of 'busbies' she had read 'breeches' and wondered on what portion of these garments a hackle could be worn.

Foreign visitors with an imperfect knowledge of English were apt unwittingly to give her opportunities for laughter of this kind. For instance, a loud-mouthed German named Von Herff came to stay at Balmoral. During an afternoon excursion with Dr. Royle he left his card at the house of the Queen's neighbour at Glenbuick. As the doctor had no card with him he turned over Von Herff's and wrote his name on the back. That night at dinner the assembled company was astonished to hear Von Herff announce: 'I left my card at Glenbuick and Dr. Royle wrote his name on my backside.' Prince John of Glucksburg was another given to making shattering pronouncements. 'Dancing like a top' was a phrase which escaped him. 'I am agreeable to see your Queen dances like a pot' was his comment when Victoria took to the floor.

When a visiting German split his Court breeches in the drawing-room she was convulsed with laughter. Lord Lawrence, on the other hand, arrived at Windsor having entirely forgotten this part of his apparel, which provoked her drily to remark 'it was a very important part of his dress, she heard, which he had left behind him'. Lord Knutsford was staying at Balmoral when it was an intimate article of female attire that enlived the evening:

> As the Queen was going out of the room she stepped on something on the floor close to the table. It turned out to be a petti-coat extender, commonly known, I believe, as a 'bustle'. Every lady present disclaimed proprietorship in it. Bigge very promptly said it did not belong to him. I said I thought it looked like Sir Henry Ponsonby's. The Queen was in fits of laughter; indeed we all were.

We had just passed into the other room when the head butler with great solemnity came in and informed us that the 'property' belonged to the Duchess (Roxburghe, I believe).

Marie Mallet later told her family of how a page then presented the bustle, 'looking like a large sausage', to the embarrassed Duchess who strenuously denied ownership. 'The Queen thereupon burst into fits of laughter.' Occasionally, though, royalty itself was liable to sartorial mishaps, as Princess Marie Louise found out:

One afternoon I was sitting in my room when I received an SOS from Her Majesty's page telling me that the Queen wished me to go to her at once. I leapt out to the corridor and found her half sitting and half lying in the passage. 'My dear, I have had a terrible accident.'

'Good heavens, what?'

Apparently the horses had shied and nearly upset the carriage and, in Grandmama's words, 'Dear Frankie Clark (who succeeded John Brown) lifted me out of the carriage and, would you believe it, all my petticoats came undone!'

CHAPTER XVIII

Indian Summer

We had a most cheerful Ladies' Dinner last night, the Queen in excellent spirits, making jokes about her age and saying she *felt* quite young and that had it not been for an unfortunate accident she would have been *running* about still! These are her very words.

This report from Marie Mallet was penned when Queen Victoria was in her eightieth year. She was in the pink of health though increasingly lame. A masseuse—known in the Household as 'The Rubber'—was engaged to knead the royal joints. The Indian servants were also helpful. With a sly smile the Queen explained: 'They are so clever when they help me out of my chair, or into a carriage, they never pinch me.'

Although dependent on her 'rolling chair' for getting about she was vain enough to dislike being seen in it in public. Indeed, in her last years she appears to have taken a belated interest in her appearance. It is true that her mantle-maker was distressed to see her leave Windsor for her Diamond Jubilee wearing her second-best mantle. But on the Jubilee Day itself her best mantle made its appearance and, as she herself recorded, she wore a new bonnet trimmed with 'creamy white flowers'. 'She is looking well and young,' reported Marie Mallet, 'and has adopted a much more becoming cap for evening wear.' On a drive to church at Balmoral Lady Lytton noticed how she took care her hair did not get ruffled. And during a drive from Osborne there was 'such laughter as we went into Ryde at the maids being vexed when the

Queen's new hat made at Windsor was put into the illustrated papers as a bonnet'.

By this time of course her mode of dress was immensely old-fashioned. Even in the 1880s one of her diplomats had been taken aback by her strange garb. 'She was dressed in a crinoline with a black silk gown in flounces which stuck out all round, with little zigzags of jet, and she looked like an old angel!' At Court the retention of other old habits produced some odd side-effects. Evening dress was worn for instance at Court entertainments and Esher noticed that the aged Queen herself wore 'an unusually low gown': *décolleté* evening dresses had been regulation evening wear at Court when she came to the throne. Then no less important a person than Albert had admired her shoulders when she wore low-cut gowns. True, after his death she had vowed never to wear them again, but this was one resolution among many she had made at that time that were quietly laid aside. Naturally she saw to it that such things were not overdone. Yes, she told Lord Rosebery, she would open the Colonial Exhibition 'as long as I don't have to wear a low dress'. And when one of her granddaughters wore a gown she thought a bit too revealing she pointed with her fan and whispered 'A little rose in front, dear child, because of the footmen.'

In her old age annual pleasure trips abroad helped to give her a new lease of life. She would return, says Marie Mallet 'as fresh as a daisy'. 'She talked and laughed incessantly and was full of interesting people she had seen'. After sampling various spots in southern Europe—Florence, Aix-les-Bains, Biarritz—she eventually settled for the French Riviera. Her visit to Nice each spring became an event eagerly looked forward to, not only for the warm sunshine and beauty of the country-side, but also for the warmth and gaiety of the local people. On arrival she would be beaming with delight and anticipation. Her world-wide reputation, together with her antique appearance, ensured that there would be a large crowd to welcome her—in the forefront a deputation of fishwives who would present her with flowers accompanied by hearty kisses.

No longer did John Brown's insularity limit her enjoyment.

Her motto now was 'When one is in a foreign country one likes to see some life about one' and the countryside was scoured for places to visit. Monasteries and soap factories were grist to her mill. For short drives her donkey carriage was put to good use, though, as Mrs. Flower, the future Lady Battersea, found out, attendance on these occasions could be a breathless experience since the entourage trotted behind on foot. Even the Empress Eugénie was once party to this procedure, the animated Queen eventually turning round, when she received no reply to her questions, to discover Eugenie speechless for lack of breath. On longer trips of course a horse-drawn carriage was used. Even then the Queen's failing eyesight created hazards for her companions. 'She was so kind and amiable and in good spirits,' the young Czar of Russia informed his mother, 'but from time to time poked me in the eye with her parasol which was less pleasant.'

Among local festivities the Battle of Flowers at Grasse was the kind of event which afforded her most pleasure. 'Some of the masqueraders, disguised as pierrots, climbed up on the balcony, holding out money-boxes, and were duly pelted by royal hands with sweet-smelling blossoms whilst from Sir Henry Ponsonby they received more lasting tokens,' reported Mrs. Flower. All in all, 'It was a very gay scene, and afforded much amusement to the Queen, who demanded more and more flowers, until at last we had to resort to the trick of having them picked up and brought back from the street below to be flung down again.' Throughout the visits, as her detective remembered, there was a good deal of musical entertainment as well.

There were evening concerts; there were morning serenades. We lived in an atmosphere of music! The morning serenades were provided by the Neapolitan strollers, those wandering singers and guitar-players, who so picturesquely bring home to one the sun of Italy and who, in many cases, are gifted with admirable voices.

The Queen liked their songs and was amused by their animated gestures. The whole brotherhood of strummers and garden Carusos knew her partiality and of the generous fee that awaited them; and every morning, at the stroke of ten, some of them would be seen entering the grounds. They crept stealthily to a spot just under the royal balcony, when for an hour at a time they spun out their *Vorrei morir* and their *Funiculi, funicula!* with all the fervour that consumes them, their eyes—such eyes!—fixed upon the window behind which a curtain rustled and was sometimes drawn to allow a kindly approving smile to fall upon the floods of melody and vigorous chest-notes below.

At a higher artistic level, perhaps, Puccini was invited to come and play to her. Sir Arthur Sullivan played the harmonium. Sarah Bernhardt, in spite of her somewhat Bohemian private life, was invited along to act. On an improvised stage she played in Theuriet's *Jean-Marie*. It was a great success. Victoria thought her 'most pleasing and gentle' and thanked her warmly. Only one thing marred the visit: Sarah was asked to sign the wrong visitors' book and, to make matters worse, exuberantly scrawled 'Le plus beau jour de ma vie' across a whole page.

At the end of one visit Victoria arranged to present a bust of herself to the manager of her hotel. Fritz Ponsonby, who had had such bad luck with the statues at Osborne, again came into his own:

> I brought him in and presented him to the Queen, who made a very pretty speech thanking him for all he had done. I then came forward with the bust, but didn't know it was not attached to the plinth, and handing it to her to hand on to the man, the bust rolled off and fell within inches of the Queen's feet, which rather spoilt the ceremony. I was afraid she would be cross but she roared with laughter and so it passed off very well.

She still had enough confidence in Ponsonby to ask him to move her, in her chair, to another part of the room as (typically) she did not want to bother the servants. 'She sat with her feet straight out and I took a firm hold of her chair and lifted it to the place she indicated,' he later recalled. She had, perhaps, a lucky escape. 'It nearly made me laugh to find myself staggering about with the chair and the Queen in it, but mercifully I did not drop it.'

Having perhaps a presentiment that her visit to Nice in 1899 might be her last she was most reluctant to leave. 'Alas! my last charming drive in this paradise of nature, which I grieve to leave, as I get more attached to it every year.' As she wrote in the Journal she had now been keeping religiously for sixty-seven years, 'I shall mind returning to the sunless north, but I am grateful for all I have enjoyed here.' It might still have been the little girl writing an account of a 'royal progress'.

It did indeed turn out to be her last foreign visit, though before she died she was planning another. During her last years Britain was fighting a difficult war in South Africa and at first suffering serious setbacks. Not that Victoria doubted the outcome. 'Please understand that there is no one depressed in this house,' she told a visiting statesman during Black Week in 1899; 'We are not interested in the possibilities of defeat; they do not exist.' To boost morale she undertook a series of public drives through London. In private, as she put it, 'all, including myself, are working for the soldiers'. 'The Queen,' Marie Mallet confirmed, 'turns out khaki comforters as if her bread depended on it.' She had made such things during the Crimean War too, she said, though without the desired result: 'They would give them to the officers, not at all what I intended.' To make up for any deficiencies this time 100,000 tins of chocolate were despatched to South Africa as her Christmas gift to the troops.

Up to this time she had had no difficulty in keeping her spirits up. Indeed, over the years Marie Mallet had been chronicling a remarkable degree of cheerfulness and bounce for a very old lady.

1895: I drove with Her Majesty yesterday and she was most talkative and amusing, indeed Mary Hughes and I had much ado to keep from immoderate laughter.
1896: At dinner came a telegram announcing the birth of twins to Princess Margaret of Hesse. The Queen laughed very much

and is rather amused at the list of her great grandchildren being added to in such a rapid manner.

1897: I have enjoyed a long drive in the Park with the beloved Queen who was very chatty and full of interest and amusing gossip.

1898: The Queen in excellent spirits, even discussing Fashoda at length and most amusing about it all.

1899 (at the time of her 80th birthday): There were between 3,000 and 4,000 letters received on the 24th, many more than the Jubilee brought forth, the Queen is much pleased by these spontaneous outbursts of loyalty and affection and it is quite certain she has never been in better health or higher spirits during her whole long life.

It seemed as though she would go on for ever. Her interest in life appeared to be unflagging. On the eightieth anniversary of the Prince Consort's birth after first attending sports at Osborne 'she asked the people to dance and watched with pleasure'. In June 1900, when she was eighty-one, she was still indulging her operatic tastes with a performance of *Cavelleria Rusticana* and excerpts from *Carmen*. 'The opera was a great success,' Lord Esher reported, 'Calvé more flirtatious in *Carmen* than words can describe—but the Queen was enchanted with her and held her hand for a long time when speaking to her afterwards.' She was still enjoying novels. 'I have nearly finished reading Marion Crawford's *Corleone* to the Queen,' wrote Mrs. Mallet, 'and she has been as much thrilled by the story as if she were a girl of eighteen!' Hector Bolitho confirms this enthusiasm. She was, he says 'like a child over Marion Crawford's story'. 'When she drove in the afternoon, she would say to her Lady, "I am excited to arrive home, so that we can get on with it. I wonder what will happen next".'

At Balmoral, she retained her old habit of visiting the sick and the needy. But the old woman who kept the shop decided when on her death-bed that her visitor was as decrepit as she was: 'Poor old soul,' were the Queen's simple words as she left. 'Puir auld creature' was the old woman's equally apt description of her visitor. In spite of her decrepitude Victoria decided when nearly eighty-one that, instead of her annual trip to 'the sunny flowery south', she would pay her first visit to Ireland for nearly forty years. 'It is *entirely* my own idea, and I must honestly confess it is *not* entirely to please the Irish, but partly because I expect to enjoy myself!' Enjoy herself she did. Despite the long history of troubles in Ireland she was given a warm welcome. Feelings were summed up as she drove through an Irish village: 'One woman yelled "God bless the Queen" while another on the other side of the road piped up "And down with the Minister in Attendance".'

During her stay at Viceregal Lodge Cardinal Logue, the Roman Catholic Primate of All Ireland, came to dinner and was captivated by her charm. As if to confirm the Queen's life-long reservations about Protestant bishops, however, the aged Archbishop of Armagh cut a sorry figure when he came to dine.

> The dear old Archbishop [Fritz Ponsonby found] shuffled along so slowly that I saw that the Queen in her chair had nearly reached the dining-room before he had gone very far. I therefore explained to him that the Queen was waiting standing up for him to say grace. Most gallantly he responded, but in his frantic efforts to go faster he nearly fell on his nose. I caught him, and after struggling together for a few moments, we started off like two men in a three-legged race and somehow reached the dining-room, where he said grace although much blown by his efforts.

During a visit to Dublin Castle it was the, by now, reverential Royal Household that was almost caught out. After announcing that the place had not changed since her last visit the Queen took tea with the Viceroy, Lord Cadogan. At this stage Ponsonby and the other attendants wandered off.

> Suddenly a messenger arrived to tell the party to come as quickly as possible as the Queen was leaving. We all ran down the passages, the women gathering up their voluminous skirts to enable them to quicken their pace. Lady Erne, a *grande dame*

of stately appearance whom I had never seen before out of a stately walk, bunched up her skirts and ran like a hare.

The Queen probably got more fun out of visiting the zoological gardens than Dublin Castle. She still loved a lion 'and they have some magnificent specimens.' Her love of children also found expression during the visit, when she requested £5 to be sent to two little girls whose action in sending her a bunch of shamrock she found touching.

Before the return to England Ponsonby noticed how old age was beginning to show. One of his duties was to ride by her carriage during her afternoon drives through the country-side.

> The Queen often went to sleep during these hot drives, and in order that she should not be seen like this by a crowd in a village, I used to dig my spurs into the horse whenever I saw a large crowd ahead and make the astonished animal jump and make a noise. Princess Beatrice always knew that this meant a crowd, and if the Queen didn't wake with the noise, she woke her herself.

As Assistant Private Secretary Ponsonby had for some time been aware of the deterioration of the Queen's eyesight due to cataracts. Increasingly she had complained 'my eyesight is tiresomely defective for reading anything pale.' Writing (barely legibly) in mauve chalk she yearned for the 'good round distinct hand' of Lord Palmerston's days. Her secretaries in spite of some ingenuity found it increasingly difficult to keep her informed of affairs of state. More and more she came to rely on Princess Beatrice to keep her in touch with events. As the Princess was not really interested this arrangement, Ponsonby told his mother, had serious drawbacks. 'Imagine B. trying to explain the vaccination question or our policy in the East. Bigge and I may write out a long *précis* of these things but they are often not read to H.M. as B. is in a hurry to develop a photograph or wants to paint a flower for a bazaar.'

Another effect of bad eyesight was a number of cases of mistaken identity.

The first time I noticed the difference was at Balmoral when before leaving the room she said, 'Where is Fritz?' Before I could interpose, Lord Balfour of Burleigh, who was six-foot-five and weighed sixteen stone, came forward with a smile and a bow, not having heard what she said. The Queen, supposing him to be me, asked him how his mother was, which startled him considerably as his mother had been dead for years.

Sometimes there was a more serious mix-up, as when she mistook the Ambassador from the French Republic for the Ambassador from the Kingdom of Italy and asked him 'Where is your King now?'

She was in addition now becoming very tired, so that Marie Mallet, part of whose job it was to read interesting newspaper items to her late at night, began to find it more and more difficult to keep her awake. 'My evening task is now no light one, the Queen sleeps soundly and yet abjures me to keep her awake, even to shake her if necessary, this I cannot bring myself to do, so I read and rustle the paper and wriggle in my chair and drop my fan and do all in my power to rouse my Sovereign, but she would be so much better in bed and so would I!' Deterioration became more rapid after the Irish visit. In addition to the effort it took to try and keep up with her duties she was afflicted by family tragedies. In July 1900 her second son, Affie, died of cancer of the throat. Her grief was so natural, Mrs. Mallet observed. 'Tears one moment and almost a smile the next at any quaint telegrams: "Sincere condolences. Poem follows".' Shortly afterwards a favourite grandson died in South Africa. And all the while in Germany her eldest daughter the Empress Frederick was dying in great agony of cancer of the spine.

In spite of everything Marie Mallet observed the old lady trying to fight back.

The Queen has been quite angelic and does her best to keep up, but the effort is very great and cannot be good for her. The curious thing is that she said to me, 'After the Prince Consort's death I wished to die, but *now* I wish to live and do what I can for my country and those I love.'

To casual observers she appeared just the same. When her latest great-grandchild, the future Earl Mountbatten of Burma, was being christened she drove from Windsor Castle to Frogmore to take part in the ceremony. 'I gather,' Lord Mountbatten has recounted, 'that I gave an early indication of my obstreperousness by knocking her spectacles off her nose while she was holding me —but to everyone's relief she took that in good part.' There were flashes, too, of her old sense of humour, as when Marie Mallet raised a laugh by conjuring up a picture of Alick Yorke as a bishop in full canonicals. One of the last stories about her to go the rounds in London concerned the kind of *faux pas* she had always enjoyed:

When Lord and Lady Roberts went down to Windsor after his return from South Africa the Queen sent a carriage and four horses to bring them up to the Castle. One of the horses became restive and tried to bolt, causing rather a sensation among the bystanders. In the course of the interview which ensued the Queen turned graciously to Lady Roberts and said: 'I am afraid one of my horses behaved rather badly this morning.' To this Lady Roberts nervously replied, 'Oh, not at all, Madam; it was nothing. I daresay it was not accustomed to much cheering!'

The year 1901, and a new century, dawned. Queen Victoria, in her eighty-second year, struggled on. Her eyesight was in a very poor state but she comforted herself with the illusion 'no one ever remembered such cloudy days'. Now, however, she was not eating or sleeping properly. As reading normally made her sleepy she tried having Beatrice read to her in bed at night. 'But it quite failed in its object, as it only made me more wakeful.' Her condition was, in the words of Henry James, 'the simple running down of an old used-up clock'. After a last weary mid-January drive she finally took to her bed. Even now, says Princess Marie Louise, her thoughtfulness did not desert her:

The Bishop of Winchester (Randall Davidson) came to Osborne

to minister to his dying Sovereign. He had been at her bedside praying with her, and after he had left the room, she turned to Aunt Beatrice and said: 'I think I ought to see Canon Clement Smith (Vicar of Whippingham Church), otherwise he might be hurt.'

Nor, on the day before she died, did she forget the last successor to Dash in her whole long line of dogs.

During the morning she brightened up and said to Sir James Reid 'Am I better at all?' He said 'Yes', and then she eagerly asked 'Then may I have Turi? (her little Pomeranian dog)'. Turi was sent for and she eagerly held him on the bed for about an hour.

The improvement was short-lived. Gradually she lapsed into unconciousness. In a lucid moment she recognised the Prince of Wales. 'She put her arms out and said "Bertie" whereupon he embraced her and broke down completely.' His name was the last word she uttered. Her last moments reminded her son-in-law of 'a great three-decker ship sinking . . . she kept rallying and then sinking'. She died in the arms of the Kaiser, the wayward grandson who was still one of her greatest admirers.

A stunned world took time to adjust to her leaving it. Afterwards Alick Yorke, who in nearly twenty years' service had once failed to amuse her, made a sentimental journey to Windsor Castle. 'I feel continually in a dream,' he wrote sadly, 'and cannot yet realise that the beloved presence which once hallowed this spot is gone forever.' On her own death-bed the grief-stricken Empress Frederick summed up her mother more simply:

'What a Queen she was—and what a woman!'

Sources & Bibliography

Sources

The Golden Thread
Very serious or all smiles: Spender I 168.

PART ONE: WHY WE WERE NOT AMUSED

After dinner: *Notebooks* 268. Admiral: *Notes and Queries* 7th November 1942, 2nd January 1943. During lifetime: Beavan 49. Bloody ancestor: F. Ponsonby 23. American manners: Longford 420. Picnic: Marie Louise 143. Elderly pansy: Mallet XVI. Shines tremendously: ibid 24. In song: Benson 33. German Granddaughter: Pope-Hennessy *Queen Victoria* 57. Yorke inimitable: ibid 75. Convulses everybody: Mallet 65.

PART TWO: WHY WE WERE AMUSED

The Gilded Cage
Earliest recollections: *Letters* 1st Series II 11. Plump as partridge: Stockmar I 78. Wilberforce: *Diary of Royal Movements* I 13. Horror of bishops: *Letters* 1st Series II 11. Teacher's diary: Argyll *V.R.I.* 56ff. Magnificent footman: Leigh Hunt. Devotion to dolls: A. Ponsonby 50. Drive with King: *Letters* 1st Series I 10. *God Save the King*: Argyll *V.R.I.* 30. Greville at Chatsworth: Enfield I 8. North Wales: Esher *Girlhood* I 48. Slape: Greenwood 51. Boat trip: Esher *Girlhood* I 141. Feodore's children: ibid 96. Dash: ibid 64ff. Operatic and terpsichorean: *Letters* 1st Series I 79. 14th birthday: Esher *Girlhood* I 75ff. Cannot valse: ibid 190. Ascot: Argyll *V.R.I.* 49. Amused at races: Esher *Girlhood* I 100. Physics lecture: ibid 89. Mozart: ibid II 338. Concert: ibid I 116. *Anna Boulena*: ibid 93. Theatre: ibid 88, 90. *Cenerentola*: ibid 70. Lablache: ibid 156. Ferdinand and Augustus: ibid 153. Ernest and Albert: ibid 157ff.

Merry Monarch
Like a dream: Esher *Girlhood* I 201. Intitulated: Tooley 72. Bishop of London: Argyll *V.R.I.* 72. Kensington nostalgia: Esher *Girlhood* I 211. Lady Salisbury: Oman 252. David Wilkie: Tulloch 45. Lady Cowley: Gore *Creevey* 427.

Creevey presented: Maxwell *Creevey* 326. Greville's view: Greville IV 40ff. American minister's wife: Boykin 115. *Oliver Twist*: Esher *Girlhood* II 86. Horses: *Letters* 1st Series I 141, Esher *Girlhood* I 298, 293, II 15. Bolted: ibid I 223. Draughts: Maxwell *Murray* 157. Chess: Esher *Girlhood* I 225. Georgiana Liddell singing: Bloomfield I 19. First Ball: Esher *Girlhood* I 317. Dear little thing: Boykin 136. Liddell's memories: Bloomfield I 19. Till past 3: *Letters* 1st Series 178. Czarevitch: Esher *Girlhood* II 188. Melbourne on theatre: ibid 109. Opera: ibid 203, 221. Russell's girl: *Letters* 1st Series I 128. Sandwich: Erskine *Sandwich* 2. Leiningen sons: Broughton V 206. Conyngham children: Esher *Girlhood* II 75. New lady-in-waiting: Maxwell *Creevey* 324. Prorogation: Wyndham 288. Bonnets and clothes: Esher *Girlhood* I 234, 340. Sleepy: ibid 185. Henry VIII: ibid 299, 218. *Oliver Twist*: ibid II 144. *Deerbrook*: ibid 305. Archbishop of York: ibid 129. Anderson's preaching: ibid 84. Not many good preachers: ibid I 231. Dogs familiar: ibid II 93. Magnetism: ibid I 245. Dolls from Berlin: ibid 266. Duke of Orleans: ibid II 93. Demagogue Hunt: ibid I 243. Bessborough: ibid 321. Guilford: ibid 390.

Dearest Albert

Dreaded marriage: Esher *Girlhood* II 154. Albert's beauty: ibid 263. Morning dresses: Grey 223. Débuted: *Letters* 1st Series I 237. Albert dancing: Esher *Girlhood* II 264. Pastimes: ibid 265. Melbourne's cynicism: ibid 275. Confides in Melbourne: ibid 266. Proposes: ibid 268. Melbourne's coat: ibid 317. Comic part: Boykin 244. Albert trying: Fulford *Dearest Child* 354. Latent fun: Argyll *V.R.I.* 54. Little small talk: Lindsay 34. Balmoral servant: Humphrey 50. Sunny face: *Letters* 1st Series II 274. Loving smile: Grey 355. Merry glee: Boykin 250. Caricatures: Wyndham 307. Polkaing: Bloomfield I 123. Told good stories: Erskine *Twenty Years* 48. Liddell examples: Bloomfield I 95. Palace concert: Lee 119. Hobhouse disapproval: Broughton VI 145ff. Matinées: Disher 196. Tom Thumb: Barnum 257ff. Coburg visit: Bolitho *Prince Consort* 80. Opera dancer: Wyndham 354.

High Life at Court

Nursing mother: (G. W. E. Russell) 291. Drawing Rooms: Marie Louise 63. Adelaide shocked: Esher *Girlhood* II 220. Barnum: Barnum 258. Clown: Wallett 67. Adelaide's standards: Boykin 45. Melbourne's view: Esher *Girlhood* I 280. Talked of Uncle: ibid II 259. Guizot: Tooley 136. Lady A.: *Letters* 1st Series 257. Day of the Lord: Bolitho *Further Letters* 95. Not admirer: Fulford *Dearest Child* 188. Dance in tent: A. E. Knight 218. False notion: *Letters* 1st Series III 290. Perfect cruelty: Connell 202. Freezing looks: James 122. Duchess of Kent: Erskine *Twenty Years* 361. Blind Hookey: ibid 360. Cards substituted: *Letters*

1st Series II 463. No fancy: ibid 322. Commerce: Erskine *Twenty Years* 26. Gladstone in net: Bassett 53. Rabusse: ibid 70. Riddles: Broughton VI 11. *Beef and Orange*: Erskine *Twenty Years* 114. French plays: Fulford *Dearest Child* 183. Reviving drama: Bolitho *Further Letters* 15. Rachel: *Letters* 1st Series II 365. Lind: ibid III 144. Les Huguenottes: ibid 2nd Series III 459. So dull Mary: M. Ponsonby 9. Warwick cried: Erskine *Twenty Years* 113. Macaulay stories: Trevelyan 549. Wellington: Wyndham 396. Uncle Cambridge: ibid 403. Gibson: Mills *Halls* 98. Measuring mouth: Lady of the Court 140. Thorburn: Erskine *Twenty Years* 157.

Happy Families

Abstractedly: Fulford *Dearest Child* 191. Capital nurse: *Letters* 1st Series I 255. Flounces: Erskine *Twenty Years* 79. Dr. Prätorious: Lady of the Court 96. Fretful at bedtime: Wyndham 336. Winter: ibid 326. Kites: ibid 403. Snowman: McLintock 36. Pocket-handkerchief: *Private Life*. Children's ball: A. E. Knight 183. Queen fussing: Erskine *Twenty Years* 258. Gladstone's daughter: Masterman 26. Royal formula: Argyll *Passages* 70. Arthur miserable: McLintock 39. Second birthday: Fulford *Dearest Child* 178. Tableau: Erskine *Twenty Years* 255ff. Nude Artemis: Mackenzie 277.

The Changing Scene

Wimpole Ball: *Diary of Royal Movements* 255. Stafford House: Argyll *V.R.I.* 240. Warwick Castle: Warwick 1. Irish jigs: *Leaves from a Journal* 261. Lovely women: *Letters* 1st Series III 267. North Terrace: Wyndham 282. Move my seat: Bloomfield I 76. Take this Miss: Jerrold 187. Sentry: Gore *George V* 16. Canrobert: Saunders 55. Consumed rings: Esher *Girlhood* II 127. Grace and dignity: Maxwell *Clarendon* II 91. Walking in heat: ibid 90. Polka: *Private Life* 134. Dogs: Saunders 153. *Jeune filles*: *Leaves from a Journal* 120. Delighted, enchanted: *Letters* 2nd Series III 172. Empress charming: Bolitho *Further Letters* 86.

Discovering Scotland

Beamingly happy: St. Helier 21. Teaching reels: Erskine *Twenty Years* 48. Blair Atholl: *Leaves from a Journal* 50ff. Albert to brother: Jagow 392. Such high spirits: Bloomfield I 125. Scotland far preferable: Wyndham 392. Malmesbury at Balmoral: Malmesbury I 345ff. Wasps' nest: *Leaves from a Journal* 143. Alfred's fall: *Letters* 1st Series III 389. Rosebery's taste: F. Ponsonby 15. Tartanitis: Maxwell *Clarendon* II 128. Highlanders amusing: *Leaves from a Journal* 169. John Brown: Fulford *Dearest Child*. Edinburgh servant: Barnett Smith. Motherliness: Lindsay 41. Church dog: ibid 107. Visiting clergyman: ibid 100. Incognito expedition: *Letters* 1st Series III 407. Lord and Lady Churchill: *Leaves from a*

Journal 194. Return in high glee: Laughton II 51. Spartan fare: *Leaves from a Journal* 226. Dear paradise: ibid 158. Wishing for snow: ibid 167.

The Last Years with Albert

Radiant happiness: Argyll *Autobiography* I 341. Chinaman: Reid *Playfair*. American soap: Greenwood 267. Smile of recognition: ibid 274. Touched: Malmesbury II 24. Trooping the Colour: *Letters* 3rd Series I 499. *Esprit de corps*: A. Ponsonby *Ponsonby* 27. Irish member: Connell 265. Queen as M.P.: ibid 219. Papa on virtues: Fulford *Dearest Child* 37. Odious report: ibid 90. Aldershot: ibid 77. Dancing score: Lee 269. Von Moltke: ibid 273. Informal dancing: Fulford *Dearest Child* 122, 271. Shuttlecock: Kinloch Cooke I 353. Theatre: Fulford *Dearest Child* 35, 233, 305. *Barchester Towers*: ibid 164. *Adam Bede*: ibid 217. *Mill on the Floss*: ibid 283. H. B. Stowe: Fields 219, 225. Victor Emanuel: Erskine *Twenty Years* 303. Esterhazy: Kennedy 63. Clarendon on Siamese: Maxwell *Clarendon* II 157. Birthday book: F. Ponsonby 37. Ibrahim Pasha: Connell 34. Unlike Continental Sovereigns: Hohenlohe-Schillingfuerst I 87. No fixed mask: Bunsen II 115. No company laugh: ibid II 7. Granville on Ireland: Kennedy 161. *Endymion*: *Letters* 2nd Series III 181. Funny collection: ibid 241. Queen of Naples: Fulford *Dearest Child* 286. Pompous Prussians: ibid 261. Crying: ibid 303. Albert's letter: Jagow 179. Prima donna: ibid 272. Beatrice's rhymes: Erskine *Twenty Years* 371. Delight in idea: Fulford *Dearest Child* 120. Opening Parliament: ibid 161. Christmas 1860: Dasent II 15.

The First Rays of Sunshine

How I leant: Fulford *Dearest Mama* 11. Bruce on Baby: Stanley *Letters* 146. Notty: ibid 170. Sayings: Fulford *Dearest Mama* 100. Sergeant: ibid 216, 221. Black boy: Morley II 97. Siamese twins: Fulford *Dear Letter* 231. Maoris: *Letters* 2nd Series I 101. More subtle conversation: Bailey II 100. German professor: Lee 349. Landseer: M. Ponsonby 58. Sketching: Tooley 212. London distasteful: Grey 379. Peaceful drives gone: Fulford *Dear Letter* 236. Meeting with Dickens: *Letters* 2nd Series II 9, 21. His earlier love: Foster *Life of Dickens* I 195. Corelli: F. Ponsonby 51. *Alice*: Redesdale 99. Fond of poems: Fulford *Dear Letter* 20. Lady Martin: Toynbee I 446. Tennyson's intruders: Tennyson 84. Windsor dance: Cartwright 116. Ponsonby joins in: A. Ponsonby *Ponsonby* 303. Atholl story: Lindsay 66.

Highland Charm

Homely speech: Lindsay 114. Grant on spinning: Fulford *Dear Letter* 28. Knitting: *Private Life* 224. As if Mrs. Jones: A. Ponsonby *Ponsonby* 64. Womanly kindness: Lindsay 64. Old customs: ibid 48. House-warming: Fulford *Dear*

Letter 208. Christy Minstrels: Kinlock Cooke. Gillies' ball: A. Ponsonby *Ponsonby* 122. Danced repeatedly: ibid 78. Brown in stupor: E. Sitwell 254. Rumblings: A. Ponsonby 285. Bacchanalian: F. Ponsonby 23. Fife: Portland 307. Small portion of whisky: *Private Life* 142. Gout: Duff 271. Servants' drinking: F. Ponsonby 151. Excellent breakfasts: *More Leaves.* Dunrobin: ibid 187. Inverness: ibid 189. Calvie: ibid 174. Stout Maggie: Lutyens 36. Dogs: *More Leaves* 67, 96, 181. Russell on her writing: Graves 130. Beerbohm: D. Cecil 374.

Man Appeal

General Gardiner: F. Ponsonby 96. Train journeys: Neele 489, 491. Duke of Cambridge: Petrie *Scenes* 211. Quoting Brown: F. Ponsonby 96. Nasty beggars: Fulford *Dear Letter* 50. Hotel tout: Tisdall *John Brown* 185. Disliking tea: A. Ponsonby *Ponsonby* 127. Kissing hands: Monypenny *Letters* IV 592. Kindest of Mistresses: *Letters* 2nd Series II 322. Length of foot: A. Ponsonby *Ponsonby* 245. Subtle beast: Maxwell *Clarendon* II 342. Admiration: Bolitho *Further Letters* 165. Lady at dinner: Marie Louise 26. Gladstone not agreeable: Fulford *Dear Letter* 248. Buckle on flattery: Monypenny & Buckle VI 462. Full of poetry: Fulford *Dear Letter* 176. Exhausted his wit: Monypenny & Buckle VI 464. Her children laughing: Monypenny *Letters* I 227. We authors: Blake 493. Loosening of etiquette: Zetland I 129, 258. Esher analysis: *Quarterly Review,* April 1901. *Coningsby: Letters* 2nd Series II 643. Don't want flattery: ibid 3rd Series I 148. Understood me: Bolitho *Further Letters* 146.

Friendly Relations

Writing to daughter: Fulford *Dearest Child* 327. More stationary: *Letters* 2nd Series I 369. Sale of letter: Mills *Two Victorian Ladies* 117. Interest in Arthur: McLintock 30, 95, 202. Leopold's learning: ibid 31. Like Chinese: Fulford *Dearest Child* 308. Mourn to music: Wilson 136. Presents: *More Leaves* 248, Fulford *Dear Letter* 308. Aching with laughter: Bolitho *Restless Years* 208. Table punishment: *Private Life* 27. Poor bit of a thing: *Letters* 2nd Series III 592. A fairy: Fulford *Dear Letter* 65. Puny children: ibid 186. Louise very ugly: Marie Louise 20. Davidson's disapproval: Bell I 95. Prince Henry: Carey 107. Mary Bulteel: M. Ponsonby XI. *Sotto voce*: ibid 15. Changing name: F. Ponsonby 45. Empress's funeral: A. Ponsonby *Ponsonby* 146. Duke of Cumberland: ibid 151. Damned if she would: ibid 64. Trousers: ibid 390. Dear General Grey: ibid 36. Unnecessary marriage: *Letters* 2nd Series I 113. Dreaded goodbyes: Waddington 369. Begging maid's pardon: *Letters* 1st Series I 19. Arthur at Balmoral: Bolitho *Restless Years* 182. Forgiving humble people: ibid 208. Papa's gardrobier: Fulford *Dearest Child.* Drunken footman: Bolitho *Victoria* 51.

Moving with the Times

First music: Stanley *Later Letters* 112. *H.M.S. Pinafore*: Bolitho *Reign* 286. Renewed dancing of valse: *Letters* 2nd Series II 615. Electric light: *Letters* 3rd Series II 294. Moving pictures: ibid III 87, 105. Chloroform: Marie I 253. Steam carriages: Esher *Girlhood* II 303 First train journey: Lee 141, *Letters* 1st Series II 507. Overnight trip: Fulford *Dearest Child* 208. Sea legs: *Letters* 2nd Series II 563. Horrible motors: Portland 316. Ambassador on smoking: Eckardstein 43. W.C. on door: Mills *Two Victorian Ladies* 117. Son-in-law's victory: F. Ponsonby 17. Lady Milford Haven: Duff 188. Soldiers in Egypt: Childers. Early dislike of heat: *Letters* 1st Series I 227. Equator argument: A. Ponsonby *Ponsonby* 115. Empress seeing ice: Carey 92. Footbath: Mallet 76. Redesdale at Balmoral: Redesdale 692. Flakes in cup: Carey 324. Maids's blue face: Mallet 38. Polo: McLintock 145. W. C. euphemisms: Fulford *Dearest Child* 170. Test the height: Alice 88.

Not So Victorian

Did not go to Kirk: Pope-Hennessy *Queen Victoria* 57. Sunday tennis: Marie Louise 147. Sunday golf. F. Ponsonby 45. Derby lottery: A. Ponsonby *Ponsonby* 120. Views on devil: ibid 118. May marriages: Fulford *Dear Letter* 123. Animal side too dreadful: ibid 266. Anatomical descriptions: Esher *Girlhood* II 57. Never lose modesty: Fulford *Dearest Child* 115. Mary's questions: ibid 142. Ladies enceinte: ibid 195. Little red lump: Fulford *Dear Letter* 200. Not hating babies: ibid 18. Modern manners: Mallet 128. Disapproval of spooning: Duff 194. Czar's surprise: Bing 82. Obedient to convention: A. Ponsonby *Victoria* 137. Rigid exclusion. G. Cecil III 183. Lady Blandford: *Letters* 3rd Series I 305. Queen Isabella: Fulford *Dear Letter* 209. Berlin sensation: ibid 253. Queen Mary's cousin: Pope-Hennessy *Queen Mary* 342. Zulu joke: Bolitho *Victoria* 81. Admiral Foley: William 65. 1871 trend: A. Ponsonby *Ponsonby* 98. Panic at Osborne: ibid 115. Explanation for dislike: Carey 207. Visiting statesmen on etiquette: Wilson 135. Harcourt: F. Ponsonby 13. Eugénie's amazement: Carey. Valiant officer: Tuckerman I 308. Solicitor-General: Furniss 84. So boutonné: Lutyens 81. When she was pre-occupied: F. Ponsonby 23. Funniest life: Wilson 133. Princesses fidgety: Lutyens 34. Lady Randolph's audience: Cornwallis-West. Girlish bashfulness: Erbach-Schonberg 216. Spoke to Melbourne: Esher *Girlhood* 383. 30 years in harness: Fulford *Dear Letter* 145. Grandchildren's view: Marie I 20. Ethel Smyth: Smyth 98. Waddington on smile: Waddington 213. Debutante on smile: Macdonell 68. Lang on royal art: Lockhart 131. Von Bulow on naturalness: Bulow II 306, 319. Bright sunbeam: *London Gazette* 14/2/1896. Dislike of boredom: A. Ponsonby *Ponsonby* 106. Dunces and fools:

Letters 2nd Series III 55. People not anxious to have: A. Ponsonby *Ponsonby* 207. Unflattering photo: (Esher) *Extracts* 273. Young Lansdowne: Fulford *Dear Letter* 240. Liked Camoys: A. Ponsonby *Ponsonby* 207.

State Occasions

State Opening: *Letters* 2nd Series I 295. Blackfriars: ibid 630. Sultan: Fulford *Dear Letter* 145. Shah's habits: Corti 191. Meeting at Windsor: *Letters* 2nd Series II 259. Journal translation: Fulford *Dearest Child* 260. Exhibition visitors: *Letters* 3rd Series I 157ff. Cetewayo: ibid 2nd Series III 326. Burmese chiefs: ibid 3rd Series II 286. Iroquois: ibid 2nd Series II 467. Squashed feet: ibid III 7. African chief: Marie Louise 149. Advice to Viceroy: Rose 327. Munshi handy: *Letters* 3rd Series I 447. Rao of Kutch: ibid 324. Out of tune: ibid 325. Going up to heaven: Jersey 110. Not in position to see: Bell I 311. Wilde's party: Hart-Davis 617ff. Commons address: Newton 89. Ugly bishops: Marie Louise 146. Bishops changing: *Letters* 3rd Series I 649. Chamberlain: Petrie *Chapters* 92. Harcourt mix-up: James 324. Campbell-Bannerman: F. Ponsonby 12. Loathing Gladstone's politics: A. Ponsonby *Ponsonby* 217. Stump oratory: *Letters* 2nd Series III 539. Attempts to spare herself: ibid 396. Head on charger: Beavan 50. Appeal to Almighty: Longford 521. He-goat: Alice 76.

Command Performance

Impromptu dance: *Letters* 3rd Series I 647. Indulging in reels: A. Ponsonby *Ponsonby* 121. Mounting horse: Mallet 37. Albert Hall: A. Ponsonby *Ponsonby* 78. *Venice:* ibid 83. Curtis's band: Spender I 168. *Lohengrin: Letters* 3rd Series I 513. *The Bells:* ibid 497. *Comédie Française:* ibid II 267. Acoustics for opera: F. Ponsonby 50. Plunket Greene: Mallet: 132. *Gondoliers: Letters* 3rd Series II 17. *Cavelleria Rusticana:* ibid 80. Brilliant *Carmen:* ibid 188. Discovering plot: Marie I 255. *Messaline:* Mallet 170. Manner perfect: Lutyens 43. Irving knighthood: Stoker 240. Terry on voice: Terry 101. Kemble: A. E. Knight 80. Bigge on enjoyment: A. Ponsonby *Ponsonby* 84. Albert Victor's complaint: Pope-Hennessy *Queen Mary* 206. Campbell-Bannerman: Spender I 169. *Helping Hands*: Sutherland Gower 212. Vicky in *Caught at Last*: Pope-Hennessy *Queen Victoria* 72ff. *L'Homme Blasé* changes: A. Ponsonby *Ponsonby*. *She Stoops to Conquer*: F. Ponsonby 51. Bigge's dilemma: A. Ponsonby *Ponsonby* 84.

Gangan

Relaxed attitude: Lutyens 143. David: *Letters* 3rd Series III 84. Tableaux: ibid II 256. Childish raids: *Private Life* 28. Noisy prattle: Lady of the Court 80. I love these children: *Letters* 3rd Series II 359. Godson's visits: Mallet 56, 71, 100. Kilmarnock letter: A. Ponsonby *Victoria* 120. Little mouse under chair: Ernle

188. Hengler's Circus: Argyll *V.R.I.* 338. Pindar's Circus: Humphrey 87. Rumour on Sanger: Disher 276. Sanger's Circus: Sanger. 4th-rate circus: Mallet 161. Turning-organ: Pope-Hennessy *Queen Victoria* 357. Such simple pastimes: *Private Life* 86. Zoo visit: Mallet 161. Seven in bed: F. Ponsonby 23. Doubling up: ibid 22. Junketing: Marie Louise 143. News of King: Esher *Girlhood* I 194. American news: *Letters* 2nd Series I 265. Two horrible news: ibid 1st Series II 512. Rolling chair: ibid 3rd Series I 503, II 265, 514, III 449. Horrid Bulgarians: Hardinge 33. Transparent bishop: *Letters* 3rd Series II 59. Short and stumpy: ibid 2nd Series II 89. Weak Granville: ibid III 455, 488. Expressive speech: E. Russell II. Oil on flames: *Letters* 3rd Series III 13. Cutting replies: ibid 20. Very American: *Letters* 3rd Series II 367. Vic's Chicks: Alice 15. Osborne statues: F. Ponsonby 19ff. Liked reminiscing: A. Ponsonby *Ponsonby* 119. Carlyle: Bolitho *Victoria* 224. Landseer portrait: Gardiner I 417. Melbourne reading: Bell I 91. Reply to Wilde: A. Ponsonby *Ponsonby* 150. To Tennyson: Tennyson 84. Amused beyond endurance: *Quarterly Review* 1901. Abraham's bosom: Marie Louise 144. Lord Erroll's prayers: A. Ponsonby *Ponsonby* 60. Hackle in busbies: F. Ponsonby 75. Von Herff's card: A. Ponsonby *Ponsonby* 61. Prince John: ibid 120. Split breeches: Ormanthwaite 36. Lord Lawrence: Argyll *Passages* 355. Lost bustle: Knutsford, Mallet 7. Horses shied: Marie Louise 157.

Indian Summer

Cheerful dinner: Mallet 148. Clever Indians: Marie I 249. Becoming cap: Mallet 37. Drive to church: Lutyens 34. Maids vexed: ibid 146. Old angel: Lister 81. Little rose: Alice 6. Donkey carriage: Battersea 114, Carey 92. Czar on parasol: Bing 113. Battle of Flowers: Battersea 115. Morning serenades: Paoli 348. Bernhardt: *Letters* 3rd Series III 151. Visitors' book: F. Ponsonby 56. Carrying her: ibid 49. Sorry to leave: *Letters* 3rd Series III 357. Working for the soldiers: ibid 483. Mallet chronicle: Mallet 63, 96, 104, 143, 166. Prince's birthday: Lutyens 149. *Carmen*: Brett 265. *Corleone*: Mallet 148, Bolitho *Victoria* 242. Ireland own idea: Mallet 192. Welcome: F. Ponsonby 64, Cardinal: ibid 63. Archbishop: ibid 65. Household panic: ibid 66. Lions: *Letters* 3rd Series III 584. Shamrock: F. Ponsonby 64. Sleeping: ibid. My eyesight: *Letters* 3rd Series II 458. Mistaken identity: F. Ponsonby 58, 24. Evening task: Mallet 178. Tears and smiles: ibid 202. Fighting back: ibid 213. Mountbatten baptism: Terraine 1. Roberts *faux pas*: *Notebooks* 276. Read to in bed: *Letters* 3rd Series III 632. Thoughtfulness: Marie Louise 146. Dog: Bell I 352. Bertie: F. Ponsonby 82. 3-decker ship: ibid. Yorke's journey: Mallet 224.

NOTE: Every effort has been made to trace original sources and copyright owners.

Bibliography

Alice, H.R.H. Princess, Countess of Athlone: *For My Grandchildren*, Evans, 1966.
Argyll, Duke of: *V.R.I. Her Life and Empire*, Harmsworth, 1901.
— *Autobiography and Memoirs*, 2 vols., Murray, 1905.
— *Passages from the Past*, Hutchinson, 1907.
Bailey, John, ed.: *The Diaries of Lady Frederick Cavendish*, Murray, 1927.
Baillie, A. and Bolitho, Hector: *A Victorian Dean*, Chatto and Windus, 1930.
Barnum, P. T.: *Life of P. T. Barnum*, Sampson Low, 1855.
Bassett, A. Tilney: *Gladstone to His Wife*, Methuen, 1936.
Battiscombe, Georgina: *Queen Alexandra*, Constable, 1969.
Battersea, Constance Lady: *Reminiscences*, Macmillan, 1922.
Beavan, Arthur H.: *Popular Royalty*, Sampson Low, 1897.
Bell, G. K. A.: *Randall Davidson*, 2 vols., Oxford, 1933.
Benson, E. F.: *As We Were*, Longmans, 1930.
Bing, E. J.: *Letters of Nicholas II to the Empress Marie*, Nicolson and Watson, 1938.
Blake, Robert: *Disraeli*, Eyre and Spottiswoode, 1966.
Bloomfield, Georgiana Lady: *Reminiscences of Court and Diplomatic Life*, 2 vols., Kegan Paul, 1883.
Bolitho, Hector: *The Prince Consort and His Brother*, Cobden-Sanderson, 1933.
— *Victoria the Widow and Her Son*, Cobden-Sanderson, 1934.
— ed.: *Further Letters of Queen Victoria*, Thornton Butterworth, 1938.
— *The Reign of Queen Victoria*, Collins, 1949.
— *My Restless Years*, Max Parrish, 1962.
Boykin, Edward: *Victoria, Albert and Mrs. Stevenson*, Muller, 1957.
Brett, M. V., ed.: *Journals of Viscount Esher*, 4 vols., Nicolson and Watson, 1934.
Broughton, Lord: *Recollections of a Long Life*, 6 vols., Murray, 1911.
Bülow, Prince von: *Memoirs*, 4 vols, Putnams, 1931.
Bunsen, Baroness: *A Memoir of Baron Bunsen*, 2 vols., Longmans, 1868.
Carey, Agnes: *Empress Eugénie in Exile*, E. Nash and Grayson, 1922.
Cartwright, Julia, ed.: *The Journals of Lady Knightly of Fawsley*, Murray, 1915.
Cecil, David: *Max*, Constable, 1964.

Cecil, Lady Gwendolen: *Life of Robert, Marquess of Salisbury*, 3 vols., Hodder and Stoughton, 1931.

Childers, Spencer: *Life of H. G. E. Childers*, Murray, 1901.

Connell, Brian: *Regina v. Palmerston*, Evans, 1962.

Cornwallis-West, Mrs. George: *Reminiscences of Lady Randolph Churchill*, Edward Arnold 1908.

Corti, Egon Caesar, Count: *The English Empress*, Cassell, 1957.

Creston, Dormer: *The Youthful Queen Victoria*, Macmillan, 1952.

Cullen, Tom: *The Empress Brown*, Bodley Head, 1969.

Dasent, A. W.: *John Thadeus Delane, His Life and Correspondence*, 2 vols., Murray, 1908.

A Diary of Royal Movements, Elliot Stock, 1883.

Disher, M. W.: *The Greatest Show on Earth*, G. Bell and Sons, 1937.

Duff, David: *Hessian Tapestry*, Muller, 1967.

— *Victoria Travels*, Muller 1970.

Eckardstein, Baron von: *Ten Years at the Court of St. James's*, 1921.

Enfield, Viscountess, ed.: *Leaves from the Journal of Henry Greville*, 4 vols, Smith Elder, 1883.

Erbach-Schonberg, Princess Marie Zu: *Reminiscences*, Allen and Unwin, 1925.

Ernle, Lord: *Whippingham to Westminster*, Murray, 1938.

Erskine, Mrs. Steuart, ed.: *Twenty Years at Court*, Nisbet, 1916.

— *Memoirs of Edward Earl of Sandwich*, Murray, 1919.

Esher, Viscount, ed.: *The Girlhood of Queen Victoria*, 2 vols., Murray, 1912.

— *Extracts from Journals*, Bowes and Bowes, 1914.

Fields, Annie, ed.: *Life and Letters of Harriet Beecher Stowe*, Sampson Low, 1897.

Fulford, Roger: *Queen Victoria*, Collins, 1951.

— ed.: *Dearest Child*, Evans, 1964.

— ed.: *Dearest Mama*, Evans, 1968.

— ed.: *Your Dear Letter*, Evans, 1971.

Furniss, Harry: *Harry Furniss at Home*, T. Fisher Unwin, 1904.

Gardiner, A. G.: *Life of Sir William Harcourt*, 2 vols., Constable, 1923.

Gore, John: *Creevey's Life and Times*, Murray, 1934.

— *King George V, A Personal Memoir*, Murray, 1941.

Gower, Lord Ronald Sutherland: *Old Diaries*, Murray, 1902.

Graves, Charles L.: *Life and Letters of Sir Charles Grove*, Macmillan, 1903.

Greenwood, Grace: *Queen Victoria, Her Girlhood and Womanhood*, Sampson Low, 1883.

Greville, Charles: *The Greville Memoirs*, 8 vols., ed. by Lytton Strachey and Roger Fulford, Macmillan, 1938.

Grey, Hon. Charles: *Early Years of the Prince Consort*, Smith Elder, 1867.

Hallé, G. E. & M., eds: *Life and Letters of Sir Charles Hallé*, Smith Elder, 1896.

Hardinge of Penshurst, Lord: *Old Diplomacy*, Murray, 1947.

Hart-Davis, Rupert, ed.: *The Letters of Oscar Wilde*, Hart-Davis, 1962.

Hohenlohe-Schillingfuerst, Prince Chloduig: *Memoirs*, 2 vols., Heinemann, 1906.

Humphrey, F. P.: *The Queen at Balmoral*, T. Fisher Unwin, 1893.

Hyde, H. Montgomery: *Henry James*, Methuen, 1969.

Jagow, Kurt, ed.: *Letters of the Prince Consort 1831–1861*, Murray, 1938.

James, R. Rhodes: *Rosebery*, Weidenfeld and Nicolson, 1963.

Jerrold, Clare: *The Married Life of Queen Victoria*, Eveleigh Nash, 1913.

Jersey, Dowager Countess of: *Fifty-one Years of Victorian Life*, Murray, 1922.

Kennedy, A. L.: *My Dear Duchess. Social and Political Letters of the Duchess of Manchester*, Murray, 1956.

Kinloch Cooke, C.: *A Memoir of Princess Mary Adelaide*, 2 vols., Murray, 1900.

Knight, A. E.: *Victoria, Her Life and Reign*, Partridge, 1897.

Knutsford, Viscount: *In Black and White*, Edward Arnold, 1926.

Lady of the Court: *Victoria's Golden Reign*, R. E. King, 1897.

Laughton, J. K.: *Life and Correspondence of Henry Reeve*, 2 vols., Longmans, 1898.

Lee, Sir Sidney: *Queen Victoria*, Smith Elder, 1904.

Lindsay, Patricia: *Recollections of a Royal Parish*, Murray, 1902.

Lister, Beatrix, ed.: *Emma Lady Ribblesdale, Letters and Diaries*, Chiswick, 1930.

Lockhart, J. G.: *Cosmo Gordon Lang*, Hodder and Stoughton, 1949.

Longford, Elizabeth: *Victoria R.I.*, Weidenfeld and Nicolson, 1964.

Lutyens, Mary, ed.: *Lady Lytton's Court Diary*, Hart-Davis, 1961.

Macdonell, Lady: *Reminiscences of Diplomatic Life*, Black, 1913.

Mackenzie, Sir Compton: *My Life and Times*, Chatto and Windus, 1970.

McLintock, M. E.: *The Queen Thanks Sir Howard*, Murray, 1945.

Magnus, Sir Philip: *King Edward the Seventh*, Murray, 1964.

Mallet, Sir Victor: *Life with Queen Victoria*, Murray, 1968.

Malmesbury, Earl of: *Memoirs of an Ex-Minister*, Smith Elder, 1884.

Manson, J. A.: *Sir Edwin Landseer*, Walter Scott, 1902.

Marie, Queen of Roumania: *The Story of My Life*, 2 vols., Cassell, 1934.

Marie Louise, H.H. Princess: *My Memories of Six Reigns*, Evans, 1956.

Masterman, Lucy, ed.: *Mary Gladstone, Her Diaries and Letters*, Methuen, 1930.

Maxwell, Sir Herbert: *The Honourable Charles Murray*, Blackwood, 1898.

— ed.: *The Creevey Papers*, Murray, 1903.

— *Life and Letters of Fourth Earl of Clarendon*, 2 vols., Edward Arnold, 1913.

Mills, A. R.: *The Halls of Ravenswood*, Muller 1967.

— *Two Victorian Ladies*, Muller, 1969.

Monypenny W. F. and Buckle G. E.: *Life of Benjamin Disraeli, Earl of Beacons-field*, 6 vols., Murray, 1910–20.

Morley, John: *Life of William Ewart Gladstone*, 3 vols., Macmillan, 1903.

Neele, G. P.: *Railway Reminiscences*, McCorquodale, 1904.

Newton, Lord: *Retrospection*, Murray, 1941.

The Notebooks of a Spinster Lady 1887–1907, Cassell, 1919.

Oman, Carola: *The Gascoyne Heiress*, Hodder and Stoughton, 1968.

Ormanthwaite, Lord: *When I was at Court*, Hutchinson, 1937.

Paoli, Xavier: *My Royal Clients*, Hodder and Stoughton, 1912.

Pearson, Hesketh: *Life of Oscar Wilde*, Methuen, 1954.

Petrie, Sir Charles: *Chapters from Life*, Eyre and Spottiswoode, 1950.

— *Scenes from Edwardian Life*, Eyre and Spottiswoode, 1965.

Ponsonby, Arthur: *Queen Victoria*, Duckworth, 1933.

— *Henry Ponsonby, His Life and His Letters*, Macmillan, 1942.

Ponsonby, Frederick: *Recollections of Three Reigns*, Eyre and Spottiswoode, 1951.

Ponsonby, Magdelen, ed.: *Mary Ponsonby, A Memoir*, Murray, 1927.

Pope-Hennessy, James: *Queen Victoria at Windsor and Balmoral*, Allen & Unwin, 1959.

— *Queen Mary*, Allen and Unwin, 1959.

Portland, Duke of: *Men Women and Things*, Faber, 1937.

The Private Life of Queen Victoria by One of Her Majesty's Servants, Pearson, 1901.

Redesdale, Lord: *Memories*, Hutchinson, 1915.

Reid, Wemyss: *Memoirs and Correspondence of Lyon Playfair*, Cassell, 1900.

Richardson, Joanna: *The Pre-eminent Victorian*, Cape, 1962.

Rose, Kenneth: *Superior Person*, Weidenfeld and Nicolson, 1969.

Russell, E.: *That Reminds Me*, T. Fisher Unwin, 1899.

(G. W. E. Russell): *Recollections of One who kept a Diary*, Smith Elder, 1898.

St. Helier, Lady: *Memories of Fifty Years*, Edward Arnold, 1909.

Salisbury, Marchioness of: *A Great Lady's Friendships*, Macmillan, 1923.

Sanger, 'Lord' George: *Seventy Years a Showman*, MacGibbon and Kee, 1966.

Saunders, Edith: *A Distant Summer*, Sampson Low, 1947.

Sitwell, Edith: *Victoria of England*, Faber 1936.

Smith, G. Barnett: *Life of Queen Victoria*, Routledge, 1900.

Smyth, Dame Ethel: *Streaks of Life*, Longmans, 1921.

Spender, J. A.: *Life of Sir Henry Campbell-Bannerman*, 2 vols., Hodder and Stoughton, 1923.

Stanley, Lady Augusta: *Letters of Lady Augusta Stanley*, ed. by A. Baillie and Hector Bolitho, Cape, 1927.

— *Later Letters of Lady Augusta Stanley*, ed. by A. Baillie and Hector Bolitho, Cape, 1929.

Stockmar, Baron E. von: *Memoirs of Baron Stockmar*, 2 vols., Longmans, 1872.

Stoker, Bram: *Personal Reminiscences of Henry Irving*, 2 vols., Heinemann, 1906.

Tennyson, Charles and Dyson, Hope, eds.: *Dear and Honoured Lady*, Macmillan, 1959.

Terraine, John: *Life and Times of Lord Mountbatten*, Hutchinson, 1968.

Terry, Ellen: *The Story of My Life*, Hutchinson, 1908.

Thorndike, Russell: *Children of the Garter*, Rich and Cowan, 1937.

Tisdall, E. E. P.: *Queen Victoria's John Brown*, Stanley Paul, 1938

— *Restless Consort*, Stanley Paul, 1952.

— *Queen Victoria's Private Life*, Jarrolds, 1961.

Toynbee, William, ed.: *The Diaries of William Charles Macready*, 2 vols., Chapman Hall, 1912.

Trevelyan, Sir George Otto: *The Life and Letters of Lord Macaulay*, Longmans, 1959.

Tuckerman, C. K.: *Personal Recollections of Notable People*, 2 vols., Richard Bentley, 1895.

Tulloch, W. W.: *The Story of the Life of Queen Victoria*, James Nesbit, 1887.

Victoria, H.M. Queen: *Leaves from a Journal of Our Life in the Highlands*, Smith Elder, 1868.

— *More Leaves from a Journal of A Life in the Highlands*, Smith Elder, 1884.

— *Letters of Queen Victoria*, 1st Series, 3 vols., Murray, 1907.

— *Letters of Queen Victoria*, 2nd Series, 3 vols., Murray, 1926.

— *Letters of Queen Victoria*, 3rd Series, 3 vols., Murray, 1930.

Waddington, Mary King: *Letters of a Diplomat's Wife*, Smith Elder, 1903.

Wallett, W. F.: *The Public Life of W. F. Wallett, the Queen's Jester*, 1870,

Warwick, Earl of: *Memories of Sixty Years*, Cassell, 1917.

West, Sir Algernon, *Recollections*, 2 vols., Smith Elder, 1899.

Wilberforce, R. G.: *Life of Bishop Wilberforce*, 3 vols., Murray, 1883.

William II, Ex-Emperor of Germany: *My Early Life*, Methuen, 1926.

Wilson, John: *C. B. A Life of Sir Henry Campbell-Bannerman*, Constable, 1973.

Woodham-Smith, Mrs. Cecil: *Queen Victoria, Her Life and Times*, Vol. 1, Hamish Hamilton, 1972.

Wyndham, Hon Mrs. Hugh, ed.: *Correspondence of Sarah Spencer, Lady Lyttelton*, Murray, 1912.

Young, Kenneth: *Arthur James Balfour*, Bell and Sons, 1963.

Zetland, Marquess of, ed.: *The Letters of Disraeli to Lady Bradford and Lady Chesterfield*, Ernest Benn, 1929.

Index